T0016816

To

....

From

....

Date

....

Renae Brumbaugh Green

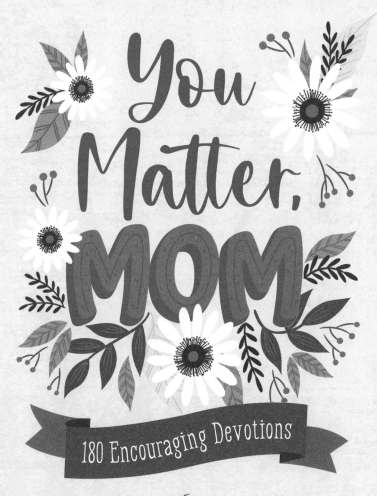

You Matter, MOM

180 Encouraging Devotions

BARBOUR
PUBLISHING

Published by Barbour Publishing, Inc., 1810 Barbour Drive, Uhrichsville, Ohio 44683, www.barbourbooks.com

Our mission is to inspire the world with the life-changing message of the Bible.

Member of the
Evangelical Christian
Publishers Association

Printed in China.

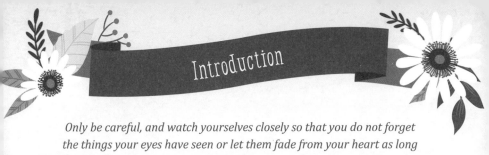

Introduction

Only be careful, and watch yourselves closely so that you do not forget the things your eyes have seen or let them fade from your heart as long as you live. Teach them to your children and to their children after them.

DEUTERONOMY 4:9 NIV

Motherhood is one of life's highest callings. Yet it's also one of the earthiest, most authentic, most basic things we women do. If the goal is to bring up competent, kind, God-fearing humans, the task can feel overwhelming. After all, the internet and social media grab for our children's attention from all sides. Can we really compete with that? Will anything we teach them actually stick?

If we rely on our own efforts, it's an uphill battle. But when we rely on God, when we seek His wisdom daily, when we live consistently in His love, He helps us. After all, He's the one who placed our children in our care, and He wants us to succeed.

The goal is not perfection—we'll never achieve it. The goal is consistency. When our children see our steady, dependable efforts to please God, when they witness our desire to imitate Him, when they experience His patience, kindness, grace, and compassion lived through us, they learn.

We teach our children not by our perfectionism but by our gritty, day-in-and-day-out consistency as we strive, fail, apologize, and try again to get it right. To live for Him. To model His love.

You were made for this, Mama. And the Holy Spirit cheers you on, coaching you through the hardest parts. Lean into Him and let His love flow through you to your children. God will honor your efforts, and your children will notice.

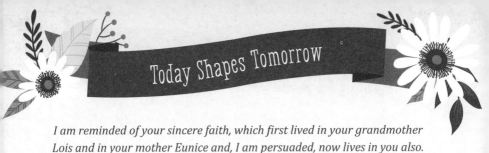

Today Shapes Tomorrow

I am reminded of your sincere faith, which first lived in your grandmother Lois and in your mother Eunice and, I am persuaded, now lives in you also.
2 TIMOTHY 1:5 NIV

· ·

Motherhood matters. But when you've gone without sleep, when there's a sink full of dishes and some gross yellow stain on your shirt, when your coffee is cold and it's been too long since you've showered, when all you want is some uninterrupted time in a nice hot bath, it's easy to question the job's value. At times like these, it's helpful to remember that motherhood is a marathon, not a sprint. The payoff comes not in a monthly paycheck but in the character of your children, as adults, who are well adjusted, kind, hardworking, and God-fearing.

That doesn't happen by accident. It happens because you, Mama, answered softly when you wanted to yell. It happens because you apologized after yelling instead of passing blame. It happens because of the little things you do, day after day, to put God first and honor Him in your home. All those little choices show your children what God's character looks like. All those little choices seep into their fiber and shape who they will become. What you do today, and every day, may seem to go unnoticed. But it will affect your children and their children and generations to come. Your faithfulness matters today. And it matters for eternity.

Lord, help me honor You in the little things.
When my children look at me, I want them to see You.

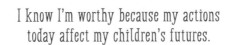

I know I'm worthy because my actions
today affect my children's futures.

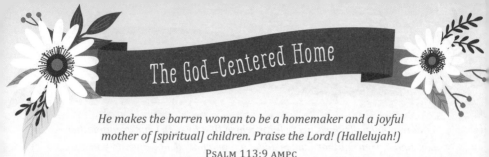

The God-Centered Home

He makes the barren woman to be a homemaker and a joyful mother of [spiritual] children. Praise the Lord! (Hallelujah!)
PSALM 113:9 AMPC

• •

The idea of a joyful mother paints such a sweet picture. But what about the frazzled mother? The sleep-deprived mother? The frustrated mother? The reality of motherhood is often far from ideal. But this verse, broken down, has some great points.

First, a homemaker makes a place feel like a home. It doesn't mean the place is always spotless, like a hospital. It doesn't mean things are perfect. When a place feels like home, it feels safe. It's a soft place to land, where you feel loved and valued.

Second, joy is different from happiness. Happy is temporary, but joyful is permanent. Happiness is based on outer circumstances, but joy is found in eternity, in the knowledge that our Savior adores us.

Finally, the phrase "spiritual children" is important. Even if a mother has a spotless home, cooks gourmet meals, and looks like a supermodel, if she fails to teach her children about God's love, they'll grow up wondering how to fill that empty place in their spirits. Spiritual children are aware of their need for God.

Mom, you matter immensely because your actions and attitudes build a safe place for your family to call home. You matter because your joy filters into your children's spirits, and your love for God shows them what the godly life looks like.

Lord, help me create a home centered around Your love.

I know I'm worthy because my actions and attitudes help build a God-centered home.

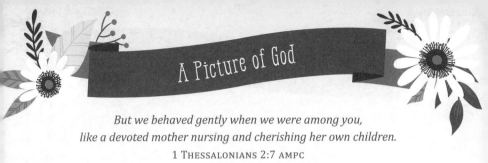

A Picture of God

But we behaved gently when we were among you,
like a devoted mother nursing and cherishing her own children.
1 THESSALONIANS 2:7 AMPC

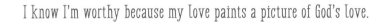

Paul was an amazing writer, known for his beautiful and relevant descriptions. It's interesting that, when trying to describe his tender love for the church at Thessalonica, he compared it to a mother's love. There's really no other picture to liken to the tender, protective, nurturing love of a mother for her child.

A mother's love, though not always perfect, is fierce. It produces superhuman strength to save a child from danger. It allows us to keep going when we're tired, to sacrifice when we want to be selfish, and to go to great lengths just to bring a smile. It was the best example Paul could think of to compare his own love for the church. It's also used in scripture to describe God's love for us.

We may not always do this mothering thing perfectly. But when we lean into God, He helps us do it well. And when we love our children with God's strength behind us, we make it easier for them to trust Him. Our tenderness paints a picture of God's tenderness. Our patience paints a picture of God's patience. And our fierce protection of them shows how God feels about each of us.

Lord, thank You for loving me with a tender, fierce love.
Show me how to love my children the way You love me.

I know I'm worthy because my love paints a picture of God's love.

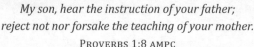

A Mother's Teaching

My son, hear the instruction of your father;
reject not nor forsake the teaching of your mother.
PROVERBS 1:8 AMPC

Solomon is known as the wisest man who ever lived. Not only was he the wealthiest man alive during his time, he was King David's son, and he wrote much of the book of Proverbs. In this verse, he encourages us to listen to our parents. After all, they love us. Even parents who aren't known for their wisdom usually try to guide their children the best they can.

But children can't learn if we don't teach them. They can't follow our instruction if we don't give it. That's why your job is so important! What you teach your children, every single day, through your choices, your words, and your actions, will seep into their minds and shape who they are.

Sometimes our children reject our teaching. Sometimes young adults choose different paths. But even if that happens, the wisdom we taught them will stay with them, like it's infused into their DNA. When we devote our parenting years to training our children in the way they should go, they will always be able to find their way back if they get lost.

Dear Father, I want to give good instruction and training to my
children. I know the best instruction comes slowly, as they watch my
daily choices. Help me model Your love and wisdom for my children.

> I know I'm worthy because my children learn by my example.

Then [Ezra] told them, Go your way, eat the fat, drink the sweet drink, and send portions to him for whom nothing is prepared; for this day is holy to our Lord. And be not grieved and depressed, for the joy of the Lord is your strength and stronghold.

NEHEMIAH 8:10 AMPC

According to Dictionary.com, the definition of joy is "the emotion of great delight or happiness caused by something exceptionally good or satisfying; keen pleasure; elation." This verse tells us the joy of the Lord is our strength. Consider that for a moment.

As parents, we often feel weary, like we can't go on. But when we delight in the Lord and take pleasure in His presence, He gives us strength. He's crazy in love with us, and He gets excited when we return the feeling. When we find joy in Him, He rewards us with strength.

Think about that newly-in-love feeling. . .the giddiness you feel. Transfer that to God, and He will energize you more than you thought possible. Sing a love song to Him. Write Him some poetry. Read His Word and soak it in, or simply feel the wind on your skin and thank Him for His kindness.

Psalm 37:4 says when we delight in Him, He'll give us the desires of our hearts. Here we see that finding joy in Him gives us strength. Find joy in the Lord today and enjoy the blessings He gives.

You are my joy and my strength, Father. I delight in You.

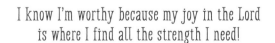

I know I'm worthy because my joy in the Lord
is where I find all the strength I need!

The Miracle Worker

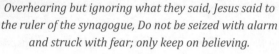

Overhearing but ignoring what they said, Jesus said to the ruler of the synagogue, Do not be seized with alarm and struck with fear; only keep on believing.
MARK 5:36 AMPC

. . . .

Jairus was a religious leader who had heard about all the miracles Jesus performed. His young daughter was sick, so he asked Jesus to heal her. But before Jesus could respond, a group showed up and said not to bother Jesus because the little girl was already dead. They clearly didn't know who Jesus really was!

Jesus ignored them and reassured Jairus. "Don't worry. Keep your faith!" He followed Jairus to his home, where people stood outside, weeping loudly. Jesus told them to stop crying because the girl was only sleeping. They laughed at Him! But Jesus ignored them, went into the girl's room, and told her to stand up. She did, and everyone witnessed God's power. Jairus' faith was rewarded.

Sometimes others may discourage your faith, telling you something isn't possible or it's unreasonable. But if you feel prompted to trust God with something big, if you feel led to ask for something bold, stay the course. Keep your faith strong and your eyes focused on Him. He is still the miracle worker.

Thank You for working large and small miracles in my life, Father. You know everything I face right now. I trust You with all of it.

I know I'm worthy because God works miracles when I follow His command to keep on believing.

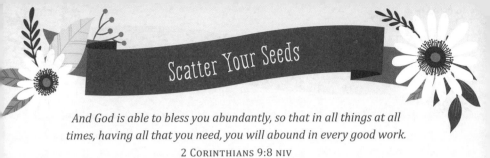

Scatter Your Seeds

And God is able to bless you abundantly, so that in all things at all times, having all that you need, you will abound in every good work.

2 Corinthians 9:8 niv

. . . .

Anyone who's tried to take family pictures knows that the more pictures you take, the better the chance of finding a few you like. The same is true for job applications—the more jobs you apply for, the greater your chances of getting hired. This is the principle Paul addresses in this verse. The more you sow, the more you reap.

God blesses us so we can bless others. That's our purpose here. Whether you're sharing money or time or talents, the more you scatter blessings on this world, the more the blessings will return to you. But here's the deal: you can't sow just so you'll reap. That kind of attitude hinders your generosity. God wants us to reach into our own seed sacks and fling those resources and abilities out into the world, without worrying about who will notice or how we'll be repaid. You do your job: bless others with your gifts, talents, and resources. Let God do His: bless you according to His great love and endless bounty. The more you give, the more He blesses. It's a win-win, no matter how you look at it.

> *Help me share the talents, abilities, and resources You've given me, Lord. I want to bless others and let them know how much You love them. Scatter my seeds, Lord.*

I know I'm worthy because God pours out His blessings on me as I sow for Him!

13

Help Me with My Doubts

Jesus said, "If? There are no 'ifs' among believers. Anything can happen."
... The father cried, "Then I believe. Help me with my doubts!"
MARK 9:23–24 MSG

A father whose son was possessed by an impure spirit approached Jesus. He had tried everything he knew to help his son, and nothing had worked. He said, "If you are able to heal my son, do it."

Jesus quickly corrected the man's attitude. "If?" He asked. "What do you mean, *if* I can do this. Do you believe in me or not?"

God's power is so much greater than our ability to understand. Sometimes, when things look bleak on our end, we question whether He can change things. When that happens, be honest with God. Like this man, tell Him that you *want* to believe. You *want* to have faith. Ask Him to heal your unbelief and show you what He can do.

What seems impossible to you right now? Ask God to make it happen, and believe with all Your heart that He is on your team. If you doubt that He can, or if you doubt that He cares enough to act, adjust your thought process and ask Him to help you overcome your doubts. He already knows what you're thinking, and He wants to help you grow in your faith.

Father, I believe You can do the impossible. Help me with my doubts!

I know I'm worthy because God helps me overcome doubts in my heart.

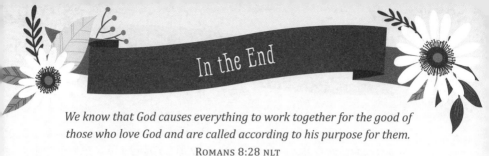

In the End

We know that God causes everything to work together for the good of those who love God and are called according to his purpose for them.

ROMANS 8:28 NLT

• •

This verse is filled with hope and confidence in God's goodness. Yet we must balance it with Jesus' words in John 16:33, where He said that in this world we will have trouble. Not everything that happens to us is good. Some things really stink, and some things will break our hearts. God didn't promise life would be easy. He promised the ultimate victory. We might think of our lives as an epic blockbuster movie. All the hard stuff we go through makes the eventual triumph even sweeter. And He will never, ever let us go through something hard without using it for something good.

For example, cancer is horrible. But a person who gets cancer will be placed in situations to share God's hope with others who may have lost hope. And the journey will teach that person and his or her family to value each moment and ignore stuff that doesn't matter. So even though it's awful, even cancer brings about good. It causes us to grow in ways that we might not have if we hadn't faced the battle.

What battles do you and your family face? Hang in there. In the end, He will work it out for good.

You know the battles I face right now, Father. I know the end of the story hasn't played out yet, and I know in the end, I'll see victory.

I know I'm worthy because God works all things for my good!

Good Works

*We are God's [own] handiwork (His workmanship), recreated in
Christ Jesus, [born anew] that we may do those good works which
God predestined (planned beforehand) for us [taking paths which
He prepared ahead of time], that we should walk in them [living the
good life which He prearranged and made ready for us to live].*

EPHESIANS 2:10 AMPC

• •

Do you remember when you first held your child in your arms? You marveled at
each precious detail—the tiny fingers and toes, the delicate eyelashes, the rosebud
lips. God looks at you the same way! You are His masterpiece, and He created you
for a purpose. He was so intentional when He thought you up that He actually
planned good things for you to do during your time here on earth.

If you're unsure about what God wants you to do, ask Him to show you. We
all have certain areas that feel more natural to us. Maybe you have the gift of
service. Look around for ways you can help. Perhaps you have the gift of mercy.
Hurting, anxious people are everywhere, and your compassion could be just
what they need. Your tender heart makes others feel less alone and gives them
courage to keep going.

God has plans for you. Ask Him what they are, and jump in.

*I want to do those things You planned for me, Father. I want to live out
Your purpose for me. Show me what You want me to do, and I'll do it.*

I know I'm worthy because God created me for good works!

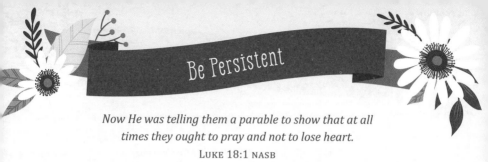

Be Persistent

Now He was telling them a parable to show that at all
times they ought to pray and not to lose heart.
LUKE 18:1 NASB

A parable is a story with a lesson, and Jesus used them often to get His message across. This parable told the story of a poor widow who kept asking a judge to help her. This judge wasn't a good, kind, God-fearing man. He ignored her time and again, but she kept coming back.

Finally, he decided to help her just to get her off his back. If a wicked judge will help bring about justice because of someone's persistence, think how much more our loving God will do for us!

Another example might be your child asking for a specific toy or opportunity. If they ask once and never mention it again, you might not think they were serious. But if they talk to you about it every day, multiple times a day, you'll understand how important it is to them. As a loving parent, you'll do your best to make it happen.

When you ask God for something, don't stop with one prayer. Show Him you mean business. Show Him that this is important to you and you know He is your only hope. Coming to Him, again and again, exhibits faith that He can change things when nobody else can.

Here is my request, Lord. You know my needs and
what I'm facing. Please respond to my prayer!

I know I'm worthy because my compassionate and loving
God hears my prayers and rewards my perseverance.

Where Are Your Eyes?

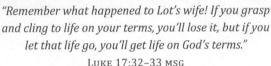

*"Remember what happened to Lot's wife! If you grasp
and cling to life on your terms, you'll lose it, but if you
let that life go, you'll get life on God's terms."*

LUKE 17:32–33 MSG

• •

Abraham's cousin Lot lived in Sodom, a city so sinful that God decided to destroy it. Abraham asked God to spare Lot and his family, so God sent some angels to warn them and help them escape. "Run!" the angels told them. "Whatever you do, don't look back."

But Lot's wife didn't really want to leave. She enjoyed her life in that sinful place. So she disobeyed the angels' command and looked back. When she did, she was turned into a pillar of salt. She disintegrated on the spot.

Living in sin always destroys us, even if it doesn't do it instantly. When we fix our gaze on things in this world instead of on God, it eats away at our spirits. Satan's goal is to ruin us, so he makes sin seem desirable.

When God says to run away from something, it's best to run. Keep your eyes on Him. He is love, and He only wants the best for your life.

*Forgive me for gazing at things I know go against Your perfect
plan for my life. Help me be sensitive to Your Holy Spirit and
obey Your voice. I want to keep my eyes on You alone.*

I know I'm worthy because God rewards me for living for Him.

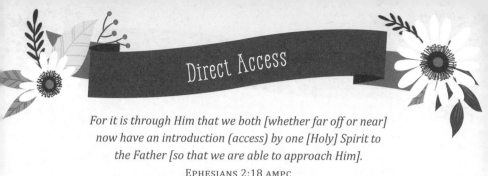

Direct Access

*For it is through Him that we both [whether far off or near]
now have an introduction (access) by one [Holy] Spirit to
the Father [so that we are able to approach Him].*
EPHESIANS 2:18 AMPC

Many moms who work or volunteer outside the home may silence their phones while they're working. We ignore telemarketers and even business calls if we're hyperfocused on a project. But if we see our child's name on the screen, most of us will answer the call no matter what. They are our most important priority.

That's how God treats us. Sure, He's got a lot going on. But unlike us, He doesn't have to juggle His priorities. He's God, and He is infinitely capable of giving each of us the attention we need. When we accept Christ and what He did for us on the cross, we become members of His family, and we have direct access to Him anytime we want. We're never a bother or a nuisance. In fact, He's delighted when we approach Him.

Take advantage of that access, today and every day. He looks forward to spending time with you, and time spent with our Father gives us strength, joy, confidence, and peace.

*Thank You for giving me direct access to You, any time I need it.
The truth is, I always need You. Teach me to pray without ceasing.
I want to walk each step of each day with You by my side, leading me.*

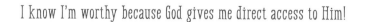

I know I'm worthy because God gives me direct access to Him!

Rejoicing over You

The Lord your God is in the midst of you, a Mighty One, a Savior [Who saves]! He will rejoice over you with joy; He will rest [in silent satisfaction] and in His love He will be silent and make no mention [of past sins, or even recall them]; He will exult over you with singing.

ZEPHANIAH 3:17 AMPC

We've all known people who like to remind us of our past failures. Perhaps it's a family member, or maybe it's a not-so-encouraging friend. They may disguise their criticism as an effort to help, but it's important to recognize the difference between genuine concern and veiled insults. A person who truly wants to support us might bring up something once, but making a habit of pointing out mistakes isn't the way God works.

When God looks at you, He sees the person you are, not the mistakes you've made. And when Christ is our Savior, we take on His righteousness. He adores you. He's excited every time you spend time with Him. He's so enamored with you, He sings love songs over you.

When you interact with your children, be an imitator of God. Focus more on who they are than on the ways they've messed up. Rejoice over them, and shower them with your love.

I want to love like You love, Father. Thank You for rejoicing over me and celebrating my existence. Help me do the same with others.

I know I'm worthy because God rejoices over me!

Believe

He is our father in the sight of God, in whom he believed—the God who gives life to the dead and calls into being things that were not. Against all hope, Abraham in hope believed and so became the father of many nations, just as it had been said to him, "So shall your offspring be."

ROMANS 4:17–18 NIV

We want to give our children the things they want. But sometimes we can't. Some things are beyond our reach. But that's not the case with God. He adores us. He created us with great purpose. He placed sacred dreams and desires inside of us, and He wants to make them come true.

God promised to make Abraham the father of many nations. When Abraham approached one hundred years (and his wife was ninety) it would have been easy to give up hope. Yet Abraham believed! He knew God could do anything. God has only to speak the word, and things happen.

What do you need God to do for you today? Is it in line with His will, His purpose, and His promises? If so, trust Him. Believe in His ability to call things into existence. Do you need a job, a car, or a place to live? Trust Him. Does peace of mind or good health seem out of reach? Hold on, believing that He will deliver. He loves you, He will take care of you, and He always keeps His promises.

All my hope is in You, Father. I believe, and I'll wait expectantly for You to act.

I know I'm worthy because God calls into being, for His beloved, things that never existed!

God Keeps His Promises

No unbelief or distrust made him waver (doubtingly question) concerning the promise of God, but he grew strong and was empowered by faith as he gave praise and glory to God, fully satisfied and assured that God was able and mighty to keep His word and to do what He had promised.

ROMANS 4:20–21 AMPC

Many years passed between the time God promised to make Abraham the father of many nations and the time Isaac was born. Most of us get impatient if we have to wait a few extra minutes for a hamburger. But as time passed, Abraham's faith grew stronger, not weaker. Instead of losing hope, he simply got more excited about what he knew God would do.

Abraham's faith put him in a right standing with God. Our Father loves faith. He loves it when we believe without doubting. He has so many good things in store for us. More than anything, He wants us to trust Him.

Is your faith waning? Think of Abraham, and give your faith a pep talk. The passing of time indicates God is working. Get excited about what He's preparing for you! Remember, He loves you more than anything. He will not let you down.

I'm sorry I've been impatient. It's so silly of me to doubt You when You've proven how amazing You are. I'm excited about what You're doing, Lord, and I can't wait to see how You'll keep Your promise to me. I know it will be great.

I know I'm worthy because God has kept His promise to me!

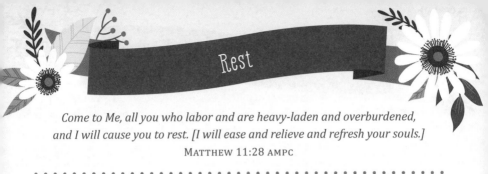

Rest

*Come to Me, all you who labor and are heavy-laden and overburdened,
and I will cause you to rest. [I will ease and relieve and refresh your souls.]*
MATTHEW 11:28 AMPC

Anyone who's parented a newborn knows the definition of weary. New parents are definitely overburdened for a while. But what about when you don't have a newborn—when nothing's causing you to feel weary, but you feel that way anyway?

The process of life can wear out our spirits. We may lie awake at night, tossing and turning, worrying about this, replaying that in our minds. We may feel sad for no obvious reason. Our muscles feel tense, and we're on edge. Life itself can be overwhelming, hard labor. But there's good news. *That's* exactly what Christ wants to relieve you of. He wants to take your burden and carry it for you.

But you have a part in the equation: "Come to Me." How often do you go to Him? How much time do you spend talking to Him in your heart, or reading His Word, or singing praises to Him? Our Lord is a gentleman in that He gives us free choice. He will not snatch our burdens without our permission. He waits for us to lay them at His feet. When we do, He will refresh us with rest and peace and joy and strength.

*Here I am, Lord. I'm exhausted, anxious, and sad. Take my burden.
. . . I give it to You freely. Thank You for giving me rest.*

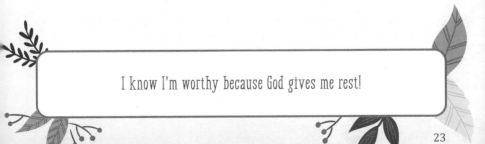

I know I'm worthy because God gives me rest!

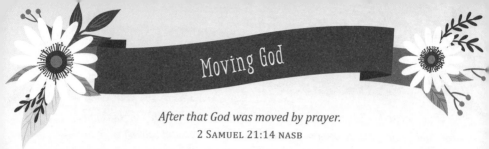

Moving God

After that God was moved by prayer.
2 Samuel 21:14 nasb

• •

It's been said that God moves mountains, but our faith moves God. When we talk to God consistently, He is impressed by our faith. He loves it when we come to Him, share our problems with Him, and trust Him with our hopes, dreams, and desires. He's not some genie in a bottle who gives in to our every whim. What He wants most is a relationship with us. When we pray, we show Him that we want that relationship too, and that touches His heart.

The more time we spend with God, the more in sync we become with His Spirit. Our desires move to mirror His desires for us. And when we tell Him what we want, and it's something He wants too, He will make it happen! He loves us, and we can be certain that if a prayer isn't answered the way we hoped, it's because He sees the bigger picture, and He has something amazing planned.

Don't lie awake worrying about things. Pray! Don't wish and daydream and hope. Pray! Your prayers move God, and He will move mountains for you.

You know what's in my heart, Lord. You know my worries,
my fears, my dreams, and my desires. I want what You want
for me, but this desire in my heart isn't going away. Please
hear my prayer and move mountains on my behalf.

I know I'm worthy because God is moved by my prayers!

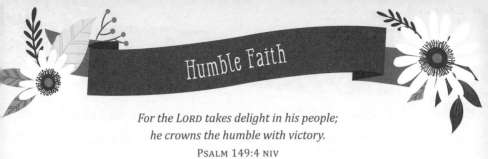

Humble Faith

For the LORD takes delight in his people;
he crowns the humble with victory.
PSALM 149:4 NIV

One of God's favorite character traits is humility. In this context, humility is a healthy understanding of who we are versus who God is. When we're in a situation that we can't control, when we know God is our only hope, *that's* humility. When we cast our cares and anxieties at His feet, expecting Him to handle them for us because we can't, *that's* humility. He loves taking care of the people who trust Him. In fact, it brings Him great joy to take care of you!

What mountain do you face? To God, it's just an anthill. What boulder stands between you and your God-given goals? To God, it's a mere pebble. Call on Him. Talk to Him. Kneel before Him, or lie face down on the floor. Pour out your heart in prayer and admit you can't do it on your own. Let Him know He's your only hope and that you trust Him completely.

This kind of attitude moves God's heart. He loves your humility and your faith. Trust Him, knowing He will act in ways You never thought possible.

Father, here I am, bowing humbly before You. I'm powerless
to make the needed changes in my life, but You are all-powerful.
I need a miracle, Lord. I need the victory that only comes from You.
I'm giving this to You, and I trust You to take care of it. I love You.

I know I'm worthy because God delights in my humble faith!

Eyes Forward

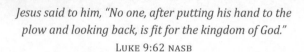

Jesus said to him, "No one, after putting his hand to the plow and looking back, is fit for the kingdom of God."
LUKE 9:62 NASB

Have you ever tried to drive your car forward while turning your head to look in the back seat? Many parents face that struggle when their children do something to distract them. The problem is clear: if you're not looking where you're going, you'll veer off course. You'll run into the ditch or a pothole. You may even crash. When driving a car, it's important to keep your eyes on the road.

The same is true for a farmer and his plow. If he wants to plow straight lines, he needs to stay focused on where he's going. If he tries to move forward while looking behind, he will zigzag all over the place. Imagine what a mess that will be at harvest time!

God wants His followers to be fully committed to Him, straight and steady, never looking back. When sin or situations pull your attention from God, discipline your mind to stay focused on Him. That's how you'll avoid wrecks and potholes. And that's when He will do great things through you.

You know I'm easily distracted, Lord. I'm sorry for taking my eyes off You. Help me stay focused, steady, and strong as I live for You. Nothing in this world matters as much to me as You do.

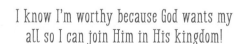

I know I'm worthy because God wants my
all so I can join Him in His kingdom!

Showers of Blessing

[My people] shall dwell safely. . .and sleep [confidently]. . . . And I will make them and the places round about My hill a blessing, and I will cause the showers to come down in their season; there shall be showers of blessing [of good insured by God's favor].
Ezekiel 34:25–26 AMPC

. . . .

Have you ever tried to count raindrops during a spring shower? It's not possible. There are too many. In the old hymn, songwriter Daniel Webster Whittle wrote, "There shall be showers of blessing/ This is the promise of love/ There shall be seasons refreshing/ Sent from the Savior above." This isn't just a pretty sentiment. It's an actual promise from God.

God adores His children. If you've chosen Christ as your Savior, you belong to Him. And He finds great delight in blessing His children, both corporately and individually.

One of the best things we can do for our mental health is practice gratitude, and God has given us so much to be grateful for. Spend some time each day counting the ways He has blessed you. You may be surprised at how long the list grows! The closer you are to Him, the more you're in His favor. No matter how bad things may seem, a survey of all the ways God has poured out His love on you serves as a great reminder of how special you are and how much He cares.

I'm overwhelmed by Your goodness, Father. Thank You for pouring out Your love on me in more ways than I can count.

I know I'm worthy because God showers me with His blessings!

No Need to Panic

*O God, have mercy on me, for people are hounding me. My foes attack me
all day long. . . . But when I am afraid, I will put my trust in you. I praise
God for what he has promised. I trust in God, so why should I be afraid?*
PSALM 56:1, 3–4 NLT

. . . .

When is the last time you felt panic? Maybe you momentarily lost your child in a
crowded shopping mall. Or perhaps your mother-in-law called, saying she was
two blocks away, and your house was a mess. The things that can induce panic are
as numerous and unique as the people experiencing it. Whether it's from a war
threat, a school shooting, or a final exam, that terrified feeling can cause our hearts
to speed up, our breathing to grow shallow, and our senses to go on high alert.

When we feel afraid, God wants us to slow down, take a deep breath, and
focus on Him. He has promised to take care of us, to never leave us or turn His
back on us. Tell Him what you're feeling and ask Him to take care of it. Then relax
into His love, breathe in His peace, and praise Him for His power.

*You know what I'm going through, Lord. Thank You
for Your promise to take care of me, no matter what.
I feel Your peace filling me now. I trust You completely.*

I know I'm worthy because God turns my panic to praise and peace!

Parting the Waters

Your path led through the sea, your way through the mighty
waters, though your footprints were not seen. You led your
people like a flock by the hand of Moses and Aaron.
PSALM 77:19–20 NIV

• •

Have you ever stood on the front side of a situation and saw no possible way through? That's how the Israelites must have felt when they were being pursued by Pharaoh's army and the Red Sea was in front of them.

Enemy behind. Deep waters ahead.

They were doomed.

But God parted the waters for them! Even with this strange miracle, it must have been terrifying to step onto that moist sand, two tall water walls looming on the right and left. If that water gave way, they'd all drown. They couldn't see God's visible footprints; they had to trust God's heart.

God still doesn't let us see His visible footprints, but we can trust His love for us. We can trust His power. And we can trust that His plans for us are good. When you're faced with an impossible situation, call to God. Then get ready for Him to show up in a mighty way. He will part waters, open doors, and lead you to safety.

I face some pretty big problems, Father. I need You to part the waters
and move the mountains. Take me by the hand and lead me to safety.
I love You, I trust You completely, and I know You are good.

I know I'm worthy because God leads me by my hand!

To Love Like He Loves

You are a God of forgiveness, gracious and merciful, slow to become angry, and rich in unfailing love. You did not abandon them.
NEHEMIAH 9:17 NLT

We all know people who have short fuses. These people are quick to anger, slow to forgive. And though they *say* they've forgiven you, they're quick to point out your past failures.

That is the opposite of God's character. He puts up with a lot from His people, and He never stops loving us or providing for our needs. Where most of us would give up and say, "I'm done," God stays and stays.

He's not a doormat. His love isn't weak. He doesn't put up with sin, and He often lets us deal with our own natural consequences when we go against His Word. But He stays with us through it all, loving us, encouraging us, and gently giving us the necessary strength and provisions to keep going.

When we repent, when we say we're sorry and that we don't want to mess up that way again, He always forgives us. And once He's forgiven us of something, He wipes our slates clean, and He never brings it up again.

Wouldn't it be great if others could say the same about us? Make it your goal to develop godly character: *forgiving, gracious and merciful, slow to become angry, and rich in unfailing love.*

Thank You for loving me no matter what,
Father. Help me love like You love.

I know I'm worthy because my God never stops loving me.

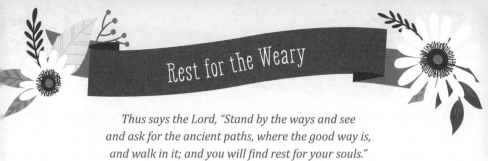

*Thus says the Lord, "Stand by the ways and see
and ask for the ancient paths, where the good way is,
and walk in it; and you will find rest for your souls."*
JEREMIAH 6:16 NASB

• •

Bone-tired is a good description for many parents, whether they have toddlers or teens. No matter if it's crying babies or car pools, a decent night's rest can seem like a distant dream. But physical exhaustion is nothing compared to a weary soul. When your body is tired, sleep is the remedy. But when your soul is tired, nothing much seems to help.

In this verse, we're told exactly what we need to do to refresh our weary souls: seek God. Ask Him to show you the way. Follow Him. Stay as close to Him as you possibly can, and you'll find your soul relaxing in His presence.

Just as it takes discipline to make sleep a priority in order to get the physical rest we need, staying close to God takes mental and spiritual discipline. We must constantly redirect our thoughts to Him. We must pray without ceasing, including Him in all our mental conversations. When we seek Him, obey Him, and cling to Him, He blesses us with joy, peace, and a renewed spirit.

*My soul is weary, Lord. Nothing I do seems to help. Show me
Your ways. Hold me in Your arms and let me feel Your presence
in my life. I need the rest that only You can provide.*

I know I'm worthy because my God provides the rest my soul craves.

Never Fear

"Don't be afraid!" Elisha told him. "For there are more on our side than on theirs!" Then Elisha prayed, "O LORD, open his eyes and let him see!" The LORD opened the young man's eyes, and when he looked up, he saw that the hillside around Elisha was filled with horses and chariots of fire.

2 KINGS 6:16–17 NLT

• •

The king of Aram wanted to ambush Israel. Time and again, his ambush failed because the prophet Elisha kept warning Israel's king. When the king of Aram found this out, he decided to capture Elisha. Elisha's servant woke up to find their home surrounded, and he was terrified. But Elisha said, "Calm down. We have an even greater army on our side." Elisha asked God to open the servant's spiritual eyes, and the young man saw God's army all around the other army.

No matter what you face, never forget you have an even greater army on your side. Ask God to open your spiritual eyes and increase your understanding. God's power surrounds and protects you. With God on your side, the victory is already yours. There's no need to be afraid, ever. You just have to believe.

Fear and anxiety have become so much a part of me, Lord, that it just feels normal. I don't want to live that way anymore. Open my spiritual eyes. Show me Your power and remind me that I don't need to be afraid.

I know I'm worthy because my God surrounds me with His power.

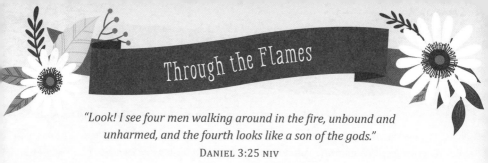

Through the Flames

"Look! I see four men walking around in the fire, unbound and unharmed, and the fourth looks like a son of the gods."
DANIEL 3:25 NIV

King Nebuchadnezzar made a law that everyone had to bow down and worship a golden image of him. When he heard that Shadrach, Meshach, and Abednego refused to do this, he threatened to throw them in a blazing furnace. Still, they wouldn't budge. They said, "We will only worship our God, who is able to deliver us from the fire. Even if He doesn't, we still won't bow down to anyone but Him."

So the king had them tossed in the fire. A while later, he looked into the furnace and saw not three but four men walking around! And there was something holy about that fourth man. . . . The Son of God Himself had joined them in the fire. The king called to the three men to come out, and they were unscathed. There was no soot, no ashes, not even the smell of smoke. Because of this miracle, Nebuchadnezzar admitted that their God was the true God. He even gave those three promotions.

When we stand up for God, He stands up for us. He walks with us through the fire and brings us out into a better place. If you're in a fire, look for Him. He is right there with you.

*Thank You for standing up for me, protecting me,
and walking with me through the flames.*

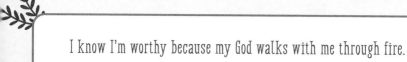

I know I'm worthy because my God walks with me through fire.

Where to Throw Your Net

They went out and got into the boat, but that night they caught nothing. . . . He [Jesus] said, "Throw your net on the right side of the boat and you will find some." When they did, they were unable to haul the net in because of the large number of fish.

JOHN 21:3, 6 NIV

After Jesus' resurrection, the disciples decided to go fishing. They fished all night with no success. The next morning, as they pulled into shore, Jesus waited for them, but they didn't recognize Him. "Catch anything?" He called.

"Nope. Not a thing."

"Throw your net to the right side of the boat."

Most men would have scoffed at that. If they hadn't met with success in deeper waters, surely there wasn't much near shore. But they had nothing to lose, so they obeyed. Sure enough, they were overwhelmed with fish.

Sometimes it's easier to scoff than to obey. After all, if nothing else we've tried has worked, why would obeying God be any different? Often God places His answers right in front of us, but we don't recognize them because we're not looking for Him.

No matter your circumstance, look for God. When You hear His voice, obey it. You have nothing to lose and everything to gain. He will always lead you to success.

Nothing I've done has led to the peace, joy, and success I long for. Show me where to throw my net.

I know I'm worthy because God uses His Word to point me to success!

He Calls You by Name

I have called you by your name; you are Mine. When you pass through the waters, I will be with you, and through the rivers, they will not overwhelm you. When you walk through the fire, you will not be burned or scorched, nor will the flame kindle upon you. For I am the Lord your God.
ISAIAH 43:1–3 AMPC

· ·

It's been said that the most precious word to any human is their own name. There's something about another person calling us by name, especially when it's done with love and fondness, that makes us feel safe, like we belong. We may "belong" to a club or organization or even a church, but if no one there knows our name, we feel out of place.

There's good news. We belong to God. Not in a corporate, fill-out-this-card-for-membership kind of way. You are His beloved child, and He calls you by name. Imagine that: the King of kings, Lord of lords, Creator of heaven and earth—He calls your name.

Not only that, but He will never leave you alone. No matter what fires you walk through or deep waters that pass over you, He will stay right by your side. He'll hold your hand, protect you, and love you through it.

Close your eyes. Listen to His voice. He loves you, and He's calling your name.

Thank You for giving me a place to belong, Father.
Thank You for knowing—and calling—my name.

I know I'm worthy because God has called me by name!

What I Have is Yours

Jesus took the five loaves and two fish, looked up toward heaven, and blessed them. . . . Afterward, the disciples picked up twelve baskets of leftover bread and fish. A total of 5,000 men and their families were fed.
MARK 6:41, 43–44 NLT

. . . .

It had been a long day for both Jesus and the disciples. A crowd of five thousand men—plus their families—were hungry for Jesus' teaching. Finally, the disciples said, "These people are hungry. Send them home to eat." Perhaps what they really meant was, "*We're* tired. Send them home."

Imagine their surprise when Jesus said, "*You* feed them."

The disciples protested, saying they didn't have the resources to feed that kind of crowd. But Jesus just told them to bring him whatever they could find. They located five loaves of bread and two fish—for thousands of people! Surely they were skeptical. But Jesus took their meager offering and turned it into a feast. There was more left at the end than what they started with.

You may feel like you don't have much to offer God. Remember, He is God. He doesn't need your time, your money, or your talent. What He really wants is your heart. When you offer Him what you have, He blesses it. He uses your humble offering to bless others and to bring Him glory. Whatever you have to offer—no matter how great or small—give it to Him.

I don't have much, Lord. But what I have is Yours.

I know I'm worthy because God blesses and multiplies my offering!

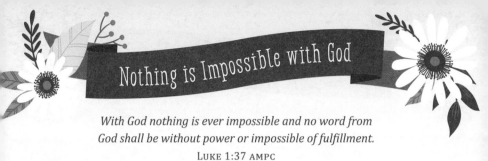

Nothing is Impossible with God

With God nothing is ever impossible and no word from
God shall be without power or impossible of fulfillment.
LUKE 1:37 AMPC

• •

Mary was just an ordinary girl. She was young and uneducated. But God saw in her the quality He most looks for in His children. She had a humble, all-consuming faith. When an angel appeared and told her she would give birth to God's Son, she didn't scoff. She didn't say, "That's ridiculous. I'm a virgin. I must be hallucinating!"

Instead, she asked a simple question—not out of doubt but just so she could better understand. "How will this happen?"

The angel explained that the Holy Spirit of God would overcome her, and this encounter would result in a divine conception of God's Son. Then the angel informed her that her older, barren cousin had also conceived. "Nothing is impossible with God," he told her.

Her reaction was the response God looks for in each of us. *I'm God's to do with as He pleases. Whatever He wants is fine with me.*

We all face circumstances we don't understand. God asks that we trust Him. He wants us to put our lives in His hands and say, "Whatever You want is fine with me." When we exhibit that kind of faith, He shows up in a big way. He moves mountains and opens doors. Nothing is impossible with God.

I'm Yours. Do whatever You want. I know nothing is impossible with You.

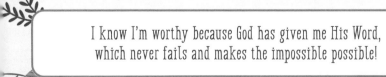

I know I'm worthy because God has given me His Word,
which never fails and makes the impossible possible!

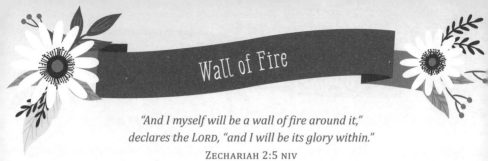

*"And I myself will be a wall of fire around it,"
declares the LORD, "and I will be its glory within."*
ZECHARIAH 2:5 NIV

. . . .

The prophet Zechariah told God's people that God would be a wall of fire around Jerusalem, protecting them from harm. He'd also be a light within them, blazing His glory for all to see. When it comes to taking care of His people, God doesn't mess around.

You're His child too. He hasn't left you to go through this life unprotected. He's a wall of fire around you and a blaze within you. On your own, you're limited in what you can accomplish. But with God, you are strong, capable, and protected.

So how do we access this kind of power? It's simple: He's already right there. We only need to look. We only need to seek Him and grab hold of Him with all our might. We do that by talking to Him (prayer) and listening to Him (reading His Word). When we spend time in His presence, we can feel that flame burning within us. Others can sense the difference around us.

When you feel alone and defenseless, remember that you're not. God's power surrounds you and His presence fills you.

*Thank You for being a wall of fire around me and a blaze
within me. I'm so grateful for Your presence in my life.*

I know I'm worthy because God and His Word are
the wall of fire around me and the flame within.

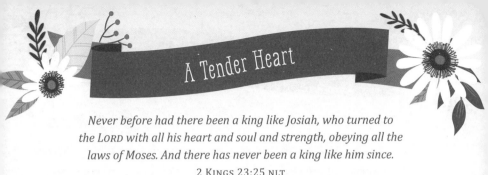

A Tender Heart

*Never before had there been a king like Josiah, who turned to
the LORD with all his heart and soul and strength, obeying all the
laws of Moses. And there has never been a king like him since.*
2 KINGS 23:25 NLT

Josiah became king of Judah at the tender age of eight. His father, Amon, was known for his idol worship. His grandfather, Manasseh, brought idols to Judah. But Josiah's great-grandfather was Hezekiah, and he was a godly king, commended for doing what was right in God's eyes.

We might wonder how a child with such a wicked father and grandfather could turn out to be a godly king. The answer is this: he had a tender heart for God. He turned to God with all his heart and soul and strength. It would have been easy for young Josiah to simply follow the path his father and grandfather had laid out for him, but he didn't. He wanted to do what was right. As he grew and learned scripture and learned how his father and grandfather had gone against God, he wept and mourned and tore his clothes.

God doesn't care about our past. He doesn't care what we've done, where we come from, or who our parents are. He cares about the condition of our hearts, right here and now. Ask yourself if your heart is tender toward God. If not, ask Him to soften it, and He will.

*I'm Yours, Lord. I want to please You. Make my
heart tender for You, and soften any hardness.*

I know I'm worthy because God favors my tender heart.

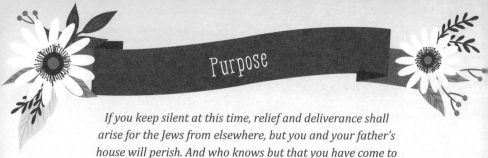

Purpose

If you keep silent at this time, relief and deliverance shall arise for the Jews from elsewhere, but you and your father's house will perish. And who knows but that you have come to the kingdom for such a time as this and for this very occasion?

ESTHER 4:14 AMPC

. . . .

Esther was raised by her cousin Mordecai. When word arrived that the king needed a new bride, he entered her in a high-stakes beauty contest. If she won, she'd be queen! Esther kept her Jewish identity a secret. Sure enough, she won the contest and the king's favor.

After she'd been queen for a time, a royal official, Haman, came up with a plan to kill all the Jews. He didn't know the queen was Jewish. Mordecai told Esther that God made her queen for this reason—to save the Jews. He knew God would deliver them, but if Esther didn't step up, she'd miss her chance to live out God's amazing plan for her life.

Though she was afraid, she trusted God. She approached the king and pled for her life and the lives of her people. Haman was punished, and the Jews were saved.

God has an important plan for your life as well. If you refuse to obey, God will find another way to do things, but you'll miss out on the blessing that comes from being obedient. Ask God to show you His purpose for your life. Then be brave, trust Him, and watch Him work.

Fulfill Your purpose in me, Lord.

I know I'm worthy because God has brought me to this time and place—for His people.

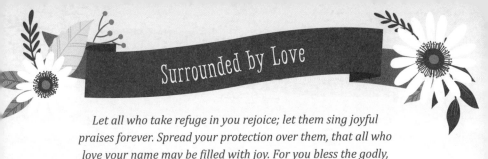

Surrounded by Love

Let all who take refuge in you rejoice; let them sing joyful praises forever. Spread your protection over them, that all who love your name may be filled with joy. For you bless the godly, O LORD; you surround them with your shield of love.

PSALM 5:11–12 NLT

Where do you run when life is too much for you? It's easy to run to a tub of ice cream, a pan of brownies, or even the Amazon shopping cart. But those things can't love you back. Those things may provide a momentary spike in feel-good hormones, but later they often leave you feeling worse than before.

When you feel stressed, anxious, or afraid, run to God. Sing to Him, for our praise draws Him near. Psalm 22:3 says God lives in the praises of His people. Think of *praise* as His address. When you're in God's presence, you feel His peace, joy, and love.

When we run to God, He surrounds us with His love like a shield. 1 John 4 tells us that God *is* love. Nothing is more powerful than that love. Run to Him, and you run straight into the center of your shield and protection. Living in the center of His love is so much more fulfilling than a pan of brownies!

I'm overwhelmed, Lord. But I will praise You in the middle of my emotion, in the middle of my crisis. Thank You for surrounding me with Your love.

I know I'm worthy because God surrounds me with His shield of love.

Stones for Success

"You come to me with sword, spear, and javelin, but I come to you in the name of the LORD of Heaven's Armies. . . ." So David triumphed over the Philistine with only a sling and a stone, for he had no sword.

1 SAMUEL 17:45, 50 NLT

• •

The entire Israelite army was afraid of Goliath. He was enormous. But David, a young shepherd boy who had fought off lions with his sling and a stone, convinced King Saul to let him have a go. Saul tried to protect David with a helmet, chain mail, and a sword, but they were too heavy. David could barely walk, much less fight, with all that stuff. So he took it all off, gathered a few smooth stones, and headed into the valley to face the giant. In the end, it only took one stone to conquer Goliath.

When we face our own giants, we often try to find security in worldly things: bank accounts, important people, or academic degrees. While none of those things are bad on their own (just as armor wasn't bad for the soldiers), God doesn't want us to place our faith in them. He's already equipped us with everything we need to succeed at the tasks He places before us. When you face difficulties, gather the stones He's given you, knowing He goes before you, He fights with you, and He will bring you to success.

Thank You for setting me up for success, Father.
I trust You alone to win my battles.

I know I'm worthy because God equips
me with everything I need to triumph.

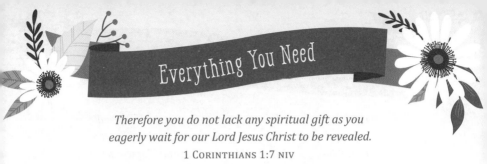

Everything You Need

Therefore you do not lack any spiritual gift as you
eagerly wait for our Lord Jesus Christ to be revealed.
1 CORINTHIANS 1:7 NIV

. . . .

When we're young, we often dream about motherhood and what that might look like. We picture happy, laughing children in clean, organized homes. We envision trips to the park, our well-adjusted children chasing butterflies and pointing out shapes in the clouds. Then reality hits, and we wonder what in the world we were thinking when we decided to become parents. Kids throw tantrums, houses get messy, and somehow motherhood doesn't look like we once thought it would. We wonder if we have the skills needed to be a good parent.

Next time you question your mothering ability, remind yourself of this verse. God has already given you everything you need to slay it in the mothering department. Motherhood isn't about clean houses or gourmet meals or even time management. It's about showing our kids how to do life when it's difficult. It's about making choices to be kind when others are mean, or working hard when you're tired. It's about love, even when love isn't the obvious response. God has given you everything you need. When you feel like you just can't, ask Him for strength, for wisdom, for patience. And remember, our purpose and calling all boils down to love.

Father, when I question my value or my ability to be a good mother,
remind me that You've already given me everything I need.

I know I'm worthy because God helps me love
my children in a way that nobody else can.

Becoming Like Jesus

And it is my prayer that your love may abound more and more, with knowledge and all discernment, so that you may approve what is excellent, and so be pure and blameless for the day of Christ, filled with the fruit of righteousness that comes through Jesus Christ, to the glory and praise of God.

PHILIPPIANS 1:9–11 ESV

Your motherhood journey is about your children, but it's also about *you*. There's nothing like a small human, totally dependent on you, to help you grow into the best (or worst) version of yourself. Just as God uses you to teach your children about His character, He uses them to teach you.

On the worst day, God will use your children to show you grace. When you struggle with pride, He'll use them to humble you. When you ask for patience, He'll let your children give you the chance to practice it. And each step along the way, you will learn to love more fiercely, more completely than you ever thought possible. The more God uses motherhood to shape you into who He created you to be, the more blessed your family will be.

Lord, my prayer is the same as Paul's. I want to love more. I want to be wise and excellent, pure and blameless. I want my life to reflect Your character. Thank You for using my children to teach me about Your love. On this journey, may we each become more like You.

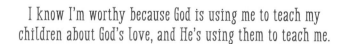

I know I'm worthy because God is using me to teach my children about God's love, and He's using them to teach me.

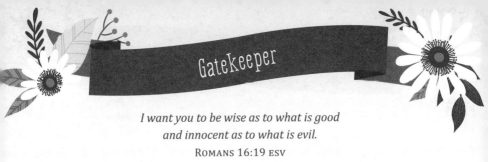

Gatekeeper

I want you to be wise as to what is good
and innocent as to what is evil.
ROMANS 16:19 ESV

Have you noticed that many kids don't seem like kids anymore? Little girls wear makeup for more than just playing dress-up at home. Boys play increasingly graphic, violent games. They're wise to worldly things far sooner than their minds and emotions are ready to process such things. You, Mama, act as gatekeeper to your child's innocence.

God wants us to be wise about what is good. That means He wants us to be patient, kind, and compassionate. He wants us to be generous; He wants us to love others. Your children will learn those things by watching you.

He also wants us to be innocent about evil. We don't have to know details about sin to recognize sin. By knowing what is good, we'll easily spot the contrast. When we watch that movie with the foul language and the graphic sex or violence, our children hear from their bedrooms. They see when they get up to get a glass of water. And something inside them thinks that stuff is okay, because Mom is doing it.

You are important to your children, today and for all the tomorrows. You are the gatekeeper of their innocence.

Dear Father, I want to be wise about what is good
and innocent about what is evil. Help me guard my
child's innocence as I teach them Your ways.

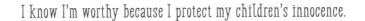

I know I'm worthy because I protect my children's innocence.

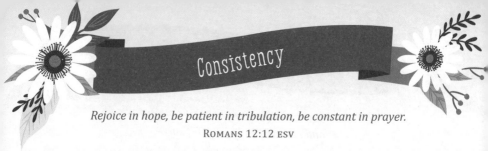

Consistency

Rejoice in hope, be patient in tribulation, be constant in prayer.
ROMANS 12:12 ESV

• •

Have you noticed that patience isn't natural for most humans? Infants scream when they're hungry. They want to be fed right now! Children fuss when they must wait their turn with a toy. Adults grumble when the grocery line is too long. Our sin nature tells us to see to our own needs without regard for others.

But when we belong to Christ, He changes our hearts, minds, and attitudes to look like His. While each heart change depends on the person, it's easier to incorporate things like joy, peace, patience, and trust in God if we've seen it modeled for us. It's okay if you don't model these things perfectly for your children. It's consistency, not perfection, that has the greatest impact.

Having a bad day? Rejoice in the hope God gives us. He is good, and He has wonderful things in store. Feeling put out? Choose to act in patience, even when you don't feel it, because that's how our Father acts toward us. Anxious and stressed? Talk to God about everything, all the time, and let your children hear you. Your consistent desire to please God, flawed though you may be, shows your children what it means to have a close, daily relationship with Him.

Lord, I know my relationship with You is far from perfect.
But I really do want to please You. Help me show my children
what it means to keep seeking You, no matter what.

I know I'm worthy because my consistent desire to please
God shows my children it's about progress, not perfection.

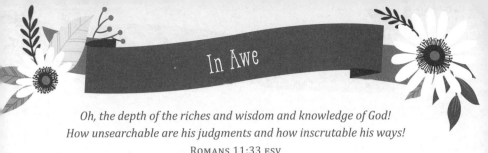

In Awe

Oh, the depth of the riches and wisdom and knowledge of God!
How unsearchable are his judgments and how inscrutable his ways!
<small>ROMANS 11:33 ESV</small>

· ·

Think back to your earliest memories of Christmas. They may be fuzzy, water-color memories, but somewhere you may recall twinkling lights, lovely carols, and brightly wrapped presents. As a small child, you probably took it all in with wide-eyed wonder, not knowing what might happen next but knowing it was sure to be amazing.

That's how God wants us to watch Him every single day. He is love. He is good and kind and generous. And He has wonderful things in store for those who love Him. His blessings and wisdom are beyond measure, and He longs for us to trust that goodness. He wants us to sit back in wide-eyed wonder, waiting to see what He'll do next, knowing it will turn out to be something incredible.

Anxiety is easy. It's often the default setting for moms. Instead of anxiety, show your children you trust Him. Model for them that wonder and expectation at His goodness. Their attitudes mimic their parents'. Show them what it looks like to trust, to believe, and to be in awe of God's goodness.

> *Dear Father, I am in awe of You. When I'm tempted*
> *to feel anxious, remind me of Your goodness. I wait,*
> *in wide-eyed wonder, to see what You'll do next.*

I know I'm worthy because I show my children
what it means to trust God's goodness.

Flaws and All

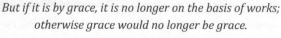

But if it is by grace, it is no longer on the basis of works;
otherwise grace would no longer be grace.
ROMANS 11:6 ESV

. . . .

Grace is such a beautiful word. It means something good that isn't deserved. Grace is the counterpart of mercy, which is withholding something bad that *is* deserved. In today's internet, social media culture, many struggle with self-worth. We compare the worst version of ourselves to others' best versions, and we come up wanting. Many have a hard time accepting God's best because they feel unworthy.

But God's love for us has nothing to do with who we are and everything to do with who He is. He loves us because He *is* love. He loves us because He created us, and we belong to Him. Our love for our children needs to model this kind of grace.

When our children think our love is tied to their performance, their talents, or their abilities, they might grow up with a messed-up idea of their worth. They may struggle to succeed, or they may give up altogether, thinking they'll never measure up. Our grace-filled acceptance of our children, flaws and all, teaches them that their worth is the same, even when they mess up. That's a message we all need to hear.

Father, help me accept Your grace. Help me love my children
with the same kind of grace, so they'll know their value.

I know I'm worthy because my acceptance
and love teach my children their worth.

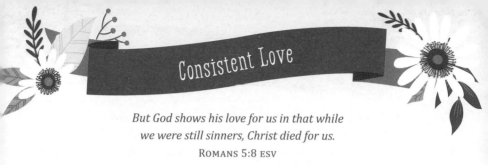

Consistent Love

But God shows his love for us in that while
we were still sinners, Christ died for us.
ROMANS 5:8 ESV

Have you ever messed up and been terrified for someone to find out? Maybe as a child, you knew your parent would be angry. Or as an adult, perhaps you forgot an important task or date, and you worried for your job or felt anxiety over your spouse's response. We all make mistakes. And we often learn the most from those who respond to those errors with grace instead of anger.

God, who is flawless, has more right than any of us to respond to our sin with harsh judgment. But that's not the way He operates. He chose us when we were a hot mess of rebellion and regret. He saw us for who we really are, and He loved us anyway. And since we're called to be like Him, that's how we should love our children.

It's easy to run out of patience and lose our cool. But that just shows our children that they're more loveable when they're at their best. The truth is, we love them the same, no matter what they do. We don't want them to say, "I messed up. I hope Mom doesn't find out." We want them to say, "I messed up. I better go tell Mom." That's the kind of love God has for us.

Lord, help me show the same love to my children whether
they behave or not. Thank You for loving me that way.

I know I'm worthy because my consistent
love teaches my children about God's love.

Grace Wins

All that passing laws against sin did was produce more lawbreakers.
But sin didn't, and doesn't, have a chance in competition with
the aggressive forgiveness we call grace. When it's sin versus
grace, grace wins hands down. All sin can do is threaten us with
death, and that's the end of it. Grace, because God is putting
everything together again through the Messiah, invites us into
life—a life that goes on and on and on, world without end.
ROMANS 5:20–21 MSG

Rules are important. So is consistency. That kind of structure feels safe and helps children learn boundaries. But sooner or later, our children will break the rules. When they do, we can either lose our temper and fly off the handle, or we can deal with the trespass with kindness, love, and compassion.

There's a difference between punishment and discipline. Punishment often deals only with the consequence of the behavior. Discipline is more concerned with what someone learns in the process. Both are important in parenting, but it's easy to have punishment without discipline. If we're not careful, we'll show anger and not grace.

But discipline allows for grace. Discipline shows a child the reason a certain action isn't okay, and it's always rooted in love. As the verse above states: "When it's sin versus grace, grace wins hands down."

Lord, help me react to my child's sin with grace. When I fail,
fill in the gaps in my child's heart and let them show grace to me.

I know I'm worthy because the way I discipline my child
paints a picture of the way God deals with all of us.

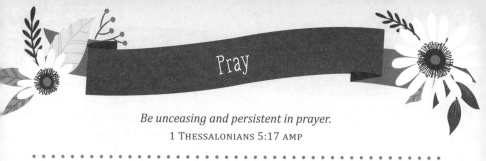

Pray

Be unceasing and persistent in prayer.
1 Thessalonians 5:17 amp

Moms are often viewed as the superheroes of childhood. We make wrong things right. We fix boo-boos, kiss hurts, and somehow know the right thing to say and do in any situation. But we all know our superpowers are limited. Good thing we know the one whose powers are limitless.

Prayer is powerful. It unleashes the strength and sovereignty of the Almighty on our behalf. Too often, we view prayer as *the least we can do.* But it's really the *most* we can do, and we have access to it every second of every minute of every day. Too often, we confine prayer to a few sentences before a meal or at bedtime. But God longs to hear from us all the time. He's interested in the details of our lives, and He longs for us to talk to Him.

Mom, your child will go through things you can't control. No matter how organized or influential you are, you can't protect your children from all the bad things in this world. But you can pray. Driving in the car? Pray. Brushing your teeth or fixing your hair? Pray. Can't sleep? Pray.

God is there. He hears. And He leans forward, anxiously waiting for you to call out to Him. Instead of relying on your own superpowers, use prayer to unleash His.

Lord, when I'm stressed or anxious, remind me to pray.
When I'm happy or sad, tired or frustrated, invite me
to pray. Thank You for the power of prayer.

I know I'm worthy because my prayers for my
children unlock God's power in their lives.

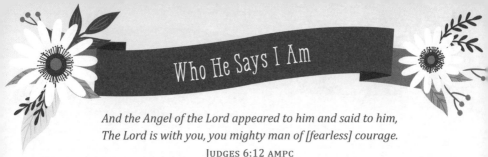

Who He Says I Am

And the Angel of the Lord appeared to him and said to him,
The Lord is with you, you mighty man of [fearless] courage.
JUDGES 6:12 AMPC

· ·

Much of motherhood takes place in private, behind closed doors. Sure, we may receive generic accolades once a year on Mother's Day, but for the most part, our contributions go unnoticed by the masses. Because of the solitary nature of our role, we may begin to doubt our self-worth. We may look in the mirror at our messy hair and baggy clothes and see ourselves as less than we are.

That's exactly what Satan wants. He whispers lies of self-doubt and disdain and convinces us they are truth. Don't be fooled. It's a trap to get us to live beneath our birthright—the birthright we received when we became His daughters. We need to tune our ears to hear what God says about us: "You are a woman of fearless courage." Without Him, we are flawed, weak, and limited. But the Lord is with us. With Him, we are righteous. We are strong. And we can do all things through Him.

We should never question God's assessment of us. If He says we're strong, we need to stop saying we're weak. If He says we're worthy, we should never tell ourselves we're worthless. We are His beloved daughters—rugged, regal, and resilient. Through Him, we are more than conquerors (Romans 8:37).

Help me see myself as You see me, Lord. I can do anything with You.

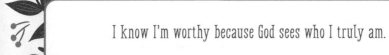

I know I'm worthy because God sees who I truly am.

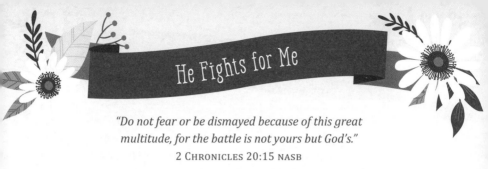

"Do not fear or be dismayed because of this great multitude, for the battle is not yours but God's."
2 CHRONICLES 20:15 NASB

In 2 Chronicles 17, we learn that King Jehoshaphat followed God, and because of that, God was with him. In this verse, enemy armies prepare to attack the king, and he was terrified. He asked God for help. He fasted and prayed. He knew he was powerless to handle the situation and that his only hope was God.

That's when God replied with the words above. "Don't be afraid, Jehoshaphat. Don't worry about a thing. This battle isn't yours to handle. It's Mine."

The king took God at His word. He led his people to stand in front of his army. They sang and praised the Lord! The enemies got confused, and they attacked each other. And Jehoshaphat gathered the spoils.

When life comes at you, when you feel surrounded and overwhelmed, seek God. When you face parenting challenges and you don't feel equal to the task, listen for His voice. He says to you, "Don't be afraid. Don't worry about a thing. This battle isn't yours to handle. It's Mine."

Take some deep breaths, remember who you are and who He is, and praise Him. He will show up, big, in the middle of that praise.

Sometimes my problems are so big, I can't see around them.
But I know You are with me, Lord, and You're fighting for me.

I know I'm worthy because my mighty God is fighting my battles.

When the Boat Rocks

But Jesus said to them, It is I; be not afraid! [I Aᴍ; stop being frightened!] Then they were quite willing and glad for Him to come into the boat. And now the boat went at once to the land they had steered toward. [And immediately they reached the shore toward which they had been slowly making their way.]
Jᴏʜɴ 6:20–21 ᴀᴍᴘᴄ

• •

In this story, Jesus has fed more than five thousand people with just a couple of fish and a few loaves of bread. You'd think His disciples would trust Him, knowing He had everything under control. But as soon as some waves rocked the boat, as soon as thunder boomed and lightning flashed, they were terrified.

We can't judge the disciples too harshly. After all, don't we do the same thing? Even though He has always taken care of our needs, we freak out when our boat is rocked. We worry that this will be the time He doesn't come through. It's important to remember that, while God is not obligated to do everything we ask Him, He is obligated to do everything He promised.

He promised never to leave us or forsake us. He promised to supply all our needs according to His riches. He promised to give us strength, to give us wisdom, and to make the path clear for those who seek Him and trust Him.

Lord, I'm sorry for the times I've doubted You.
Thank You for always taking care of me.

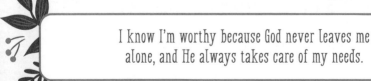

I know I'm worthy because God never leaves me
alone, and He always takes care of my needs.

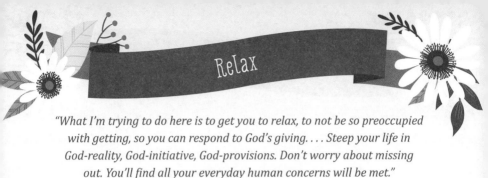

"What I'm trying to do here is to get you to relax, to not be so preoccupied with getting, so you can respond to God's giving. . . . Steep your life in God-reality, God-initiative, God-provisions. Don't worry about missing out. You'll find all your everyday human concerns will be met."
MATTHEW 6:32–33 MSG

Moms can do a lot of things. We are nurses, bus drivers, chefs, teachers, organizers, and CEOs of our family business. But relax? Relaxing can be a little challenging when you're wearing the "Mom" hat. We can become so fixated on getting everything done right that we forget we're not really the ones in charge.

God didn't intend for motherhood to be a never-ending journey of perfectionism. Our children and families are gifts, and He wants us to enjoy them, knowing He will take care of the details. Yes, we still have to be the grown-ups. But each day, before we pin on that "Mom" badge, we need to remember that we're God's daughters. We need to sit at His feet, spend time in prayer, and listen to Him speak words of love and affirmation.

Being a mom is an important job, no doubt. But our most important job is to be His child. Relax. Look to Him. He will take care of everything that matters.

Thank You, Lord, for reminding me that I'm Your child before I'm a mom and that You love me enough to take care of all my needs.

I know I'm worthy because God sees to every detail of my life better than I ever could.

He Has Your Back

*The steps of a [good] man are directed and established by the
Lord when He delights in his way [and He busies Himself with
his every step]. Though he falls, he shall not be utterly cast down,
for the Lord grasps his hand in support and upholds him.*
PSALM 37:23–24 AMPC

Each day of motherhood is filled with choices. Cereal or eggs? Watch television or play outside? Dress them or let them choose what to wear? That doesn't even include choices we make for our own lives. All those options can quickly lead to decision fatigue.

The truth is, we won't always get it right. Sometimes we will mess up. But when we love God and genuinely want to please Him, He has our backs. When we seek Him daily and try our best to live righteous, godly lives, He smooths the way for us. And when we have a bad day or make a poor choice, He picks us up, sets us on our feet, and gives us strength to keep moving forward. Even better, He will cause our mistakes to work out for good in the end.

*Sometimes I feel overwhelmed by all the daily decisions, Lord.
What if I do it wrong? What if I blow it? Thank You for covering me
with grace and for using even my mistakes in a way that leads to good.*

I know I'm worthy because God guides
my steps, supports me, and has my back.

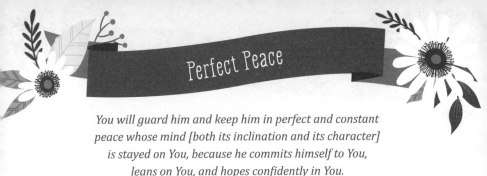

Perfect Peace

*You will guard him and keep him in perfect and constant
peace whose mind [both its inclination and its character]
is stayed on You, because he commits himself to You,
leans on You, and hopes confidently in You.*

ISAIAH 26:3 AMPC

Most moms are great worriers. We don't mean to be, but our children give us so much to worry about. Our love for them is bigger than anything we've experienced, and we want only the best for them. We want them to be healthy. Happy. Successful. Popular. Confident. Safe. But we can't control everything in their lives, so we feel smothered by a crippling anxiety.

God wants to take our worries, our fears, and our anxieties and replace them with His perfect peace. He even tells us how to make the exchange, right in this verse. We must stay focused on Him! When we constantly turn our thoughts to God, He notices. When we lean into Him, when we place our hope in Him alone, He is impressed with our faith. He loves all His children, but He offers special blessings to those who trust Him completely.

*Lord, You know I don't mean to worry. I want to trust You with my
children, but sometimes I focus too much on what can go wrong in
their lives instead of all the wonderful things You want to do for them.
When anxiety takes over, remind me to trust You. I know You love them
even more than I do, and You have beautiful plans for their lives.*

I know I'm worthy because God cares
enough to replace my worry with peace.

57

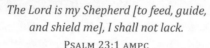

The Good Shepherd

The Lord is my Shepherd [to feed, guide,
and shield me], I shall not lack.
PSALM 23:1 AMPC

Despite a common idea that sheep are difficult animals, they are actually quite intelligent. Like humans, they form lasting relationships, stick up for their buddies in fights, and mourn when they lose a friend or family member. They experience joy, sadness, fear, boredom, and anger. It's no wonder God's Word compares Jesus to a good shepherd and us to sheep.

Like sheep, we need protection. We need food and shelter. We need someone to guide us in the right direction, away from danger—we need a shepherd. And because God is a loving parent, He provides all those things for us, just as we provide them for our own children.

Sometimes we may feel inadequate to give our children all they need. We may feel anxious about feeding them, giving them the best advice, or keeping them safe. But we can relax and trust our Good Shepherd. He loves us, and if we stay close to Him, He will care for our every need—including the need to care for our little ones.

Thank You, Lord, for being my Good Shepherd. I know You will care
for my needs, including my need to be a good mother. Thank You
for guiding me as I guide my children, protecting me as I protect
them, and for covering my entire family with Your love.

I am worthy because my Good Shepherd cares for me.

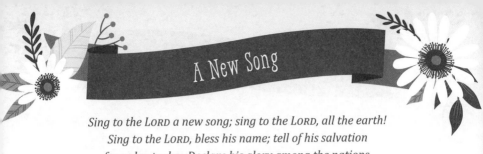

A New Song

Sing to the LORD a new song; sing to the LORD, all the earth!
Sing to the LORD, bless his name; tell of his salvation
from day to day. Declare his glory among the nations,
his marvelous works among all the peoples!

PSALM 96:1–3 ESV

One of the main reasons God created us is so we can worship Him. We were created for worship! Each day, He wants us to sing Him a new song. It doesn't have to be a *good* song, by the world's standards. Our voices don't have to be perfectly on pitch, and the words don't even have to rhyme. When we sing a new song, God thinks it's beautiful!

We worship in many ways, not just through song. We worship through our words when we tell others about how great He is. We worship through our actions when we live out His love in ways other people can feel and experience. Preparing a meal, playing on the carpet with our children, and doing laundry are all ways we sing a new song to Him, every single day. Today, instead of trying to make things perfect, ask yourself what creative thing you can do to bring God pleasure. Chances are, it will bring you pleasure as well.

Lord, make my life a song. Make each new day a verse written for Your pleasure. I want those around me to feel Your presence as I worship You.

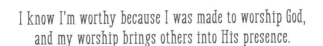

I know I'm worthy because I was made to worship God,
and my worship brings others into His presence.

Keep Talking

Hear my prayer, O LORD; let my cry come to you! Do not hide
your face from me in the day of my distress! Incline your
ear to me; answer me speedily in the day when I call!
PSALM 102:1–2 ESV

Have you ever had a day like this? The psalmist was frustrated and distressed, and he wondered if God even heard his pleas for help. He was tired of the mess he was in, and he wanted God to answer. He wanted God to fix things. Right. Now.

One of the hardest lessons of the Christian life is that God is God and He is under no obligation to do things on our timeline. He doesn't have to answer right away. He's not required to consult with us about what He's doing or how long it will take.

But He is bound by each of His promises. He promised that He will never leave us. That means even when we don't think God is anywhere around, He's right there. He promised He will never forsake us. So when it feels like every circumstance is designed to knock us down, God is in control, and the outcome will be good.

When life hits hard, keep praying, even if it feels like those prayers aren't being heard. Later in this chapter, the psalmist writes with confidence: "He regards the prayer of the destitute and does not despise their prayer" (verse 17 ESV). Keep talking. He is listening. And He is working on your behalf.

Lord, thank You for hearing me. Show me You're working. I trust You.

I know I'm worthy because God always hears my prayers.

For the Future

But the steadfast love of the LORD is from everlasting to everlasting
on those who fear him, and his righteousness to children's children,
to those who keep his covenant and remember to do his commandments.
PSALM 103:17–18 ESV

• •

Everlasting to everlasting—that sounds like language from a fairy tale. It means there's no beginning and no end. That's how big His love is for those who fear Him! He's not obligated to those who don't regard Him, who don't try to live their lives to please Him. But for those of us who treat Him with reverence and respect, for those who care what He thinks and do our best to live for Him, the blessings are far reaching and unending.

Think about that. Our actions today affect today. But they also affect the future, just as our grandparents' actions affected our lives. God isn't concerned about perfection. He knows who we are, and He knows our flaws. He's more concerned with consistency. When we keep going, trying to show His love, trying to model kindness and compassion for our children, trying to put others first and leave each person feeling a little more encouraged and cared for than when we met them. . .when we make daily choices to honor Him. . .He is pleased. He blesses us. And He pours out that bucket of blessings into future generations as well, all because we were faithful.

Father, teach me to live a reverent, holy, joyful life for You. Thank You
for blessing me and for blessing my future generations as well.

I know I'm worthy because my choices today
affect my children, grandchildren, and beyond.

A Cheerful Giver

Now I say this: the one who sows sparingly will also reap sparingly,
and the one who sows generously will also reap generously. Each one
must do just as he has decided in his heart, not reluctantly
or under compulsion, for God loves a cheerful giver.

2 CORINTHIANS 9:6–7 NASB

Most mothers do what they must to take care of their children. We feed them, bathe them, tie their shoes, and sign their permission slips. We make sure their homework is done and drive them to and from soccer games. It's one thing to do all these things. It's quite another to do them *cheerfully.*

Taking care of our children is, in many ways, an obligation. But taking care of our families with a smile on our faces and a song in our hearts is a gift. That one shift can turn a toxic environment into a haven of peace. When we do these things grudgingly, we sow sparingly. We give the minimum of what's required. But when we go about our daily tasks with love and cheer and excitement for the opportunity to bless others, we sow generously. And that kind of heart will reap enormous blessings. Our children won't always be happy, but a child who grows up in a joyful, peace-filled environment will be well adjusted, be emotionally healthy, and have an abundance of beautiful memories. That's the legacy we choose for them when we give of ourselves cheerfully.

Lord, help me do all I need to do today with a
smile on my face and a song in my heart.

> I know I'm worthy because my attitude
> builds a legacy for my children.

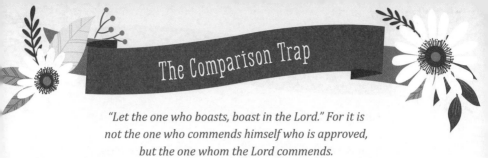

The Comparison Trap

*"Let the one who boasts, boast in the Lord." For it is
not the one who commends himself who is approved,
but the one whom the Lord commends.*
2 CORINTHIANS 10:17–18 ESV

- -

It's easy for moms to play the comparison game. We compare our children, and when our own children seem smarter, more talented, or better behaved, we feel good about ourselves. But when they come up short, we feel like bad mothers.

We compare ourselves to other moms. *Why can't I be pretty like her? Why is her house always clean and mine's always a wreck? I wish I could cook, teach, decorate, (fill in the blank) like her.*

But these kinds of comparisons are pointless and are tied to our own pride. We want bragging rights so we can feel accomplished and worthy. But pride is God's enemy. When we set ourselves up in pride, we set ourselves against God. It should never be, "Look at me." It should always be, "Look at God."

It should never be, "I'm right." It should always be, "What does God say?"

God created each of us in His image. We are His masterpieces. We're not mass-produced assembly-line products. We're one of a kind. Next time you're tempted to fall into the comparison trap, remind yourself that God loves a humble heart. If you need to brag on something, brag on Him.

*Lord, it's hard not to compare myself to others.
Forgive me for my pride. Help me compare myself
only to You, as I try to become more like You each day.*

I know I'm worthy because I am created in God's image.

Voices

Finally, brothers, whatever is true, whatever is honorable, whatever is just, whatever is pure, whatever is lovely, whatever is commendable, if there is any excellence, if there is anything worthy of praise, think about these things.

PHILIPPIANS 4:8 ESV

• •

We all have voices inside our heads. Research shows that most times, these voices are negative. This toxic self-talk can make or break a day, a week, a year, a life. God's Word tells us the source of these gloomy, defeatist thoughts is Satan. He is the Liar, and he loves to pour his lies into our minds.

The good news is that we have the power to shut up the lies. If we just tell Satan to stop, we'll be left with a void in our thought processes, and the lies will come right back. Instead, we need to replace the negative with positive. God wants us to focus on His love and His truth. He wants us to listen to His voice. Where Satan shouts, God whispers, because He is a gentleman.

When you hear that cynical voice in your head telling you you're not enough, you don't measure up, or that you've failed, tell Satan to be quiet. Call him out for his lies. Then listen for the truth: God loves you. He adores you! He created you exactly as He wanted you to be, so you can fulfill the purpose He has for your life. You are royalty, because you are the daughter of the Most High King.

Listen only to Him.

Help me recognize Satan's lies. Teach me to fill my mind with Your truth.

I know I'm worthy because God adores me.

Making Friends

*I thank my God in all my remembrance of you, always in every
prayer of mine for you all making my prayer with joy, because of
your partnership in the gospel from the first day until now.*
PHILIPPIANS 1:3–5 ESV

Remember when friendships were easier? When we were kids, we had built-in friendships through our neighborhoods, our classes, our extracurricular activities, and our churches. Though they weren't always perfect, there always seemed to be something to do or somebody to hang out with.

When adulthood hits, those opportunities for friendship aren't created for us. We have to be intentional or they won't happen. Even though we have responsibilities and chores and families who depend on us, we still need to connect with other women. We need friends. And that means we must create a culture and climate in which friendships can grow.

It might mean inviting people over, even when the house is a mess. It might mean staying longer at that playdate with the other moms, even though you have errands to run. It might mean looking outside your normal parameters for friends, crossing cultural, economic, and age barriers.

When we invest in friendship, we invest in people. And the return on those investments is often our greatest source of blessing.

*Lord, I know You created us for relationships. Remind me to nurture
old friendships and develop new ones. Help me be a blessing to others.*

I know I'm worthy because my gift of
friendship is a blessing to others.

Writing Your Story

And I am sure of this, that he who began a good work in you will bring it to completion at the day of Jesus Christ.

PHILIPPIANS 1:6 ESV

- -

When we're in the middle of it, the long season of motherhood seems to go on forever, with little hope of ever escaping the piles of dishes and mounds of laundry and endless shuttle services from one extracurricular event to another. But ask any mother of adults, and she'll tell you that busy season of childhood lasts only a breath. Blink, and it's gone.

In those moments when all your days blur together in a gray smudge of sameness, remember that there is great purpose in each dish wiped and each towel folded. God is doing a work in you, and this is just part of the process. Like a runner must train by running laps, and a weight lifter gets stronger by doing reps, we grow more like Him with each passing day that we seek Him and serve Him by serving others.

This season won't last. For those who are faithful, we will one day look back and see what we can't see now: God is writing our story. He's not finished yet. But we can know, with confidence, that it will be an amazing one.

Sometimes it feels like You're not doing anything, Lord.
My days run together, and I feel like nothing I do matters.
Remind me that this season is important, both for me and for
my children, as You work to make each of us more like You.

> I know I'm worthy because God is
> writing an amazing life story for me.

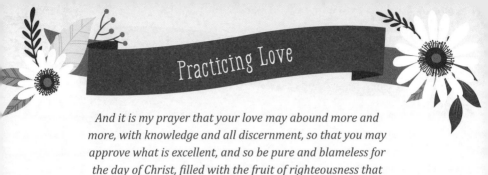

Practicing Love

And it is my prayer that your love may abound more and more, with knowledge and all discernment, so that you may approve what is excellent, and so be pure and blameless for the day of Christ, filled with the fruit of righteousness that comes through Jesus Christ, to the glory and praise of God.

PHILIPPIANS 1:9–11 ESV

If you've ever listened to an accomplished pianist or watched a professional basketball player in action, you know that person didn't arrive at their current level of greatness overnight. Many people show promise and skill, but it's only those who persevere, who practice for days and months and years, who truly excel.

You may have one or more areas of giftedness. You may even have some things you're truly great at. But there's one thing, more than any other, that God wants us to excel at. He wants us to love! And the only way we will get to the pro level is to practice. To push. To love even when it's hard, even when we don't want to love.

Love means showing patience when we're at the end of ourselves. It means being kind when others aren't. It means acting in humility when our pride is wounded. Love—the real, deep, pro-level kind of love—goes against our human nature. But love is the very essence of who God is, and He wants us to be like Him.

Help me to love like You love, Lord. When love is hard, remind me that it's an opportunity to practice, to improve, and to become more like You.

I know I'm worthy because I can love like God loves.

Back to Life

Then he said to me, "Prophesy over these bones, and say to them,
O dry bones, hear the word of the Lord. Thus says the Lord God
to these bones: Behold, I will cause breath to enter you, and you
shall live. And I will lay sinews upon you, and will cause flesh to
come upon you, and cover you with skin, and put breath in you,
and you shall live, and you shall know that I am the Lord."

Ezekiel 37:4–6 esv

Motherhood is a blessing. But with it comes some things that don't feel like blessings, like the loss of personal identity. Before we were mothers, we were interesting people with hobbies and talents and sought-after skills. Now we clean toilets and wipe poopy diapers in our free time.

If we're honest, we'll admit that in some ways, we feel like we've lost ourselves, like our former existence is gone. If we're not careful, our spirits can become dry and brittle.

But God created *you*! You're not a cookie-cutter, assembly-line kind of mom. You're unique, and God wants you to flourish. He wants your spirit—the part of you that makes you *you*—to be alive in every way.

His Word gives life. If you feel dry and brittle, read His Word. Talk to Him. Sing to Him. Wrap your arms around His neck and cuddle Him close. His presence will bring skin and flesh to your bones, and you'll feel more alive than ever.

Stay close to me, Lord. Breathe life into my spirit.

I know I'm worthy because God brings my dry spirit back to life.

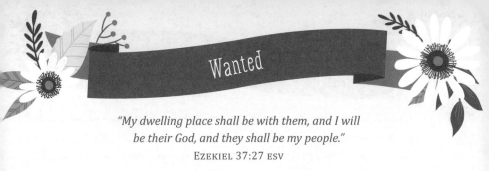

Wanted

*"My dwelling place shall be with them, and I will
be their God, and they shall be my people."*
EZEKIEL 37:27 ESV

. . . .

Before we had children, we had visions of what parenthood would be like. We pictured ourselves playing in the yard or cuddled on the couch reading books. Maybe we envisioned time in the kitchen, baking and decorating cookies. Most of us probably *didn't* see ourselves hiding out in the bathroom with little fingers poking under the crack in the door, asking how long till we're done. And we certainly didn't dream of being eternally judged by harsh teenage critics.

Being a mom has its tough moments, for sure, but most of us want the same things. We want to have good relationships with our children. And we want them to be happy and safe and productive.

That's how God sees us. He longs for a close relationship with us. More than anything, He wants us to spend time with Him. He wants to see us living out the peace and joy He provides. He wants us to feel a sense of purpose as we carry out His plan for our lives. He loves us so much He prepared a beautiful home for us in heaven. For now, while we wait, He offers to move right into our hearts.

It's a wonderful thing, really, to be so *wanted*.

*Lord, remind me when I can't find any alone time that
my children want to be with me because they love me
so much. I know You long for my presence as well.*

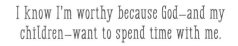

I know I'm worthy because God—and my
children—want to spend time with me.

God's Powerful Daughter

Now it was Mary Magdalene and Joanna and Mary the mother of James and the other women with them who told these things to the apostles, but these words seemed to them an idle tale, and they did not believe them.

LUKE 24:10–11 ESV

• •

In recent times, the women's movement has brought attention to injustices faced by women everywhere. This is nothing new. Throughout time, women have been disregarded by some. There will always be those who discredit women simply because of our gender.

One thing is certain: God does not underestimate His daughters. Despite cultural norms, women in the Bible are consistently given leading roles in His story. After Jesus' death, women cared for His body. Women made sure He was treated with the dignity and respect He deserved. And women discovered the empty tomb!

It was women who spread the word that Jesus' body was no longer there, that He had risen, just like He said. Though most of the apostles doubted their story, Peter listened. And Peter saw for himself that these women knew what they were talking about.

Don't ever let anyone underestimate you because of your gender. And don't ever underestimate yourself either. God certainly doesn't.

Thank You for reminding me that You made me powerful and important. Help me act in the strength You've already given me.

I know I'm worthy because God calls me His daughter.

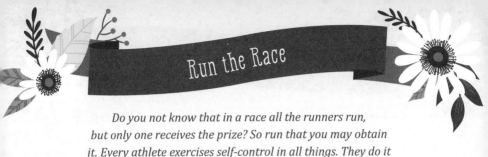

Run the Race

Do you not know that in a race all the runners run,
but only one receives the prize? So run that you may obtain
it. Every athlete exercises self-control in all things. They do it
to receive a perishable wreath, but we an imperishable.
1 CORINTHIANS 9:24–25 ESV

We moms have a thousand little distractions, every single day. Whether it's battles over what's for breakfast or if it's okay to wear snow boots in July or setting an appropriate curfew, it can be hard to stay focused on the ultimate goal. We forget there even is a goal, beyond getting through the day.

But the goal is this: we want our children to grow into kind, compassionate, God-fearing people who love the Lord and serve others with their gifts. Whew! That's a big goal. That's why it's important to stay focused on that.

Don't be overwhelmed by the magnitude of the task. Just ask yourself, each day, *How can I model kindness? How can I teach compassion? How can I show my children that pleasing God is more important than pleasing others?*

Aside from a handmade Mother's Day card, we probably won't win a physical prize this side of heaven. But the outcome of bringing up children who love God with all their hearts and want to serve Him will impact generations to come, into eternity.

Lord, help me keep my eye on the prize. Give me wisdom and
self-discipline as I run this motherhood marathon with purpose.

I know I'm worthy because I'm running a race that affects eternity.

Run with Purpose

So I do not run aimlessly; I do not box as one beating the air.
But I discipline my body and keep it under control, lest after
preaching to others I myself should be disqualified.
1 CORINTHIANS 9:26–27 ESV

Paul had a lot of wisdom to give his readers. He wanted to make sure they knew he practiced what he preached. If he had required one thing of his audience yet didn't require it of himself, he would have lost credibility.

It's easy for parents to require one thing of their children but do another. "Because I said so" is a common answer we give. Whether or not our children are obedient in the moment, they learn more from our actions than from our rules. If we tell them not to say unkind things but they overhear us gossiping, they will grow into gossips. If we punish them for using foul language, but we use those same words, they will add those words to their vocabularies.

If we want our children to respect our rules, we need to respect them ourselves. They may not always do what we say, but our example will make a deep impression on the people they will become. As we model kindness, patience, compassion, and love, we make it easier for them to develop and emulate those traits.

I need Your help, Lord, as I practice what I preach.
I want to model godly behavior for my children.

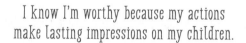

I know I'm worthy because my actions
make lasting impressions on my children.

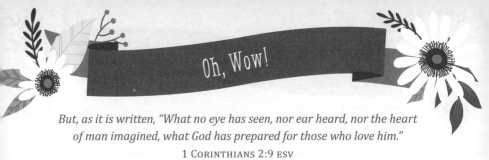

Oh, Wow!

But, as it is written, "What no eye has seen, nor ear heard, nor the heart of man imagined, what God has prepared for those who love him."

1 CORINTHIANS 2:9 ESV

It would be nice if our children arrived with instruction manuals—each one unique, with its own set of information about how to best parent this particular model. Since no such manual exists, we do the best we can. We read books. We ask for advice. When all else fails, we do what others are doing, just in case they know something we don't.

God doesn't want us to rely on human wisdom for parenting, or for anything else. What He has for us is so much better than what our logic can figure out. It's good to read books and seek wise counsel, but our primary sources of wisdom should be God's Word and prayer. His ways don't always make sense on the front end. But when we seek and obey Him, we will come out on the other side saying, "Wow. I had no idea He was doing this."

God is bigger and greater than we can truly understand this side of heaven. He has amazing things in store for those who love Him and consistently follow His ways. Trust Him. Trust the process. And get ready to be awed.

Thank You for the wonderful, amazing things I know You have in store for me and my family. When I'm not sure what to do, remind me to look for answers in Your Word and trust You.

I know I'm worthy because God has amazing things planned for me.

Not Perfect

Those of crooked heart are an abomination to the LORD, but those of blameless ways are his delight. Be assured, an evil person will not go unpunished, but the offspring of the righteous will be delivered.
PROVERBS 11:20–21 ESV

None of us is perfect, aside from Christ. We will make mistakes. We will goof up. In the course of our lives, we'll each have thousands of things we wish we could go back and do differently. But God is okay with imperfection. He's not okay with sin, but He knows us. He created us. He's never had any delusions about who we are. And He knows there's a difference between a pure heart that makes mistakes and an evil person. He wants us to honestly look at ourselves. When we mess up, He wants us to say we're sorry and move on with trying to please Him.

When we do this, we are called "blameless." Not because we're perfect but because Christ took the blame from us. When we consistently try to please Him, we're called "righteous," and He promises to bless our children on our behalf.

Forget about perfectionism. It's overrated and impossible to attain this side of glory. Instead, focus on consistent effort to honor God, to love others, and to shine His light in this world.

Thank You for this reminder that I don't have to be perfect.
Give me a pure heart, and make me blameless in Your sight.

I know I'm worthy because God sees me as righteous, and He will bless my children because of my efforts to please Him.

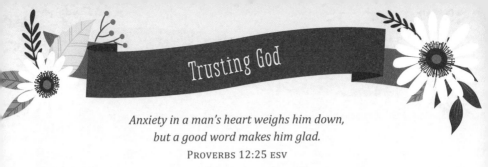

Trusting God

Anxiety in a man's heart weighs him down,
but a good word makes him glad.
PROVERBS 12:25 ESV

Mothers are notorious worriers. After all, motherhood is a big responsibility. What if we get it wrong? And what about the times we can't be there to protect our children? There's so much to be anxious about, but God's Word tells us in Philippians 4:6 (ESV), "Do not be anxious about anything, but in everything by prayer and supplication with thanksgiving let your requests be made known to God."

When we allow anxiety to rule our thoughts, words, and actions, we run the risk of passing those anxious tendencies to our children. After all, they mirror our attitudes. When you're tempted to worry, follow Paul's advice: Pray. Give thanks. Tell God what You want. Remind Him—out loud—of all His promises. After all, God isn't obligated to do what we ask, but He *is* obligated to keep His Word.

By quoting scripture, we speak positive words over the situation. God's words hold power, so let your children hear you quoting scripture out loud. In doing so, you'll relieve some of your own fears. And you'll give them powerful tools to apply to their own anxious situations, every day of their lives.

Thank You for this reminder that anxiety is useless. When I
feel anxious, help me trust You. Help me live out my faith in
You in a way that teaches my children to trust You too.

I know I'm worthy because I can teach my children how to trust God.

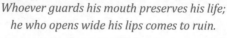

*Whoever guards his mouth preserves his life;
he who opens wide his lips comes to ruin.*
PROVERBS 13:3 ESV

It's easy—too easy—to let our guards down in front of our children. We say things we shouldn't say, because we forget that little people have big ears. Whether we use language we shouldn't, say unkind things about others, or express anxiety over a situation, our words have a big impact on our family's mental health and well-being.

It's tempting to just close the door and say what we want to say out of their hearing. But inevitably, our words will come back to us. Guarding our tongues is hard work. It's a discipline, for sure. In James 3, the author spends several paragraphs talking about the tongue. His point is this: none of us will ever gain full control over our tongues, but we should still try.

Our words can be used as weapons or devices of healing. They can hurt others or bless them. It's worth it to put in the hard work needed to make sure we don't destroy those we love with our own lips. If you're not sure you can speak words that honor God and build others up, stay quiet. To the best of your ability, only say words that breathe love and life and blessing.

*Lord, help me edit my words before they leave my mouth.
I only want to say things that honor You and bless others.*

I know I'm worthy because my words have the power to bless others.

Every Single Day

Because of the LORD's great love we are not consumed,
for his compassions never fail. They are new every
morning; great is your faithfulness.
LAMENTATIONS 3:22–23 NIV

• •

Sometimes the magnitude of our work as mothers can feel overwhelming. All the little day-to-day tasks scream to be dealt with, and in the midst of laundry and car pools and healthy meal prep and work obligations, we're supposed to be intentional about raising kind, compassionate, productive, God-fearing humans.

It's a lot.

But God never asked us to do it all at once. He just wants us to take it one day, one step, at a time. Each morning, ask Him to walk with you through your day. Trust Him to help you complete the tasks that need to be completed. Seek Him for wisdom for this moment, this situation. That's all He requires.

Be fully His, right now. Be kind. Loving. Faithful. Compassionate. Right now.

Then trust Him for the next hour, the next day, the next month. Minute by minute, day by day, He provides what we need. Moment by moment, He guides those who seek Him. He loves us deeply, and He is faithful. He never fails.

Lord, thank You for a fresh start, a new beginning each day. Give me
wisdom and strength, courage and compassion, for this moment. Hold
my hand and guide my steps as I love You and love my family well.

I know I'm worthy because God gives me what I need, every single day.

Quiet Expectation

I say to myself, "The LORD is my portion; therefore I will wait for him."
The LORD is good to those whose hope is in him, to the one who
seeks him; it is good to wait quietly for the salvation of the LORD.
LAMENTATIONS 3:24–26 NIV

• •

In what do you place your hope? Modern society sends many different messages. Some say our hope is in education. Others stress the importance of retirement funds. Still others claim all our problems will diminish if we just eat organic foods.

Education, financial planning, and healthy eating are all good choices, but they're not where our hope lies. James 1:17 says that every good and perfect gift comes from God. He is the source of all we need. He loves us, and He longs to bless those who trust Him alone.

It's easy to *say* we trust Him and then try to manipulate things to turn out the way we want them to. But that's not really trust. That's not really hope. Because hope is believing good things are in store and acting in accordance with that belief. He wants us to wait in quiet expectation—not throwing a fit and not trying to control the outcome. He wants us to believe so much in His perfect plan that we calmly go through our days in wide-eyed expectation of the good things He will do.

I trust You, Lord. I'm excited to see the good things
You have in store for me and my family.

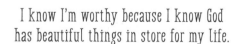

I know I'm worthy because I know God
has beautiful things in store for my life.

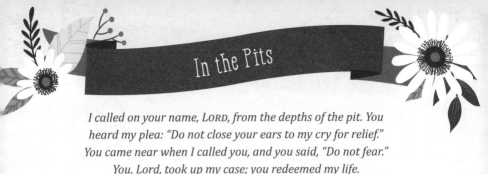

In the Pits

I called on your name, LORD, from the depths of the pit. You heard my plea: "Do not close your ears to my cry for relief." You came near when I called you, and you said, "Do not fear." You, Lord, took up my case; you redeemed my life.

LAMENTATIONS 3:55–58 NIV

Have you ever had one of those in-the-pit days? Of course you have. We've all had those weeks, months, and even years. Humorist Erma Bombeck wrote an entire book on this topic titled *If Life is a Bowl of Cherries, What Am I Doing in the Pits?*

Life isn't about staying out of the pits. We'll all end up there, no matter what we do to avoid it. That's why God's Word gives us instructions for what to do in those moments.

Talk to God! Call out to Him. Tell Him exactly what you're feeling. Don't hold back. After all, He already knows what you're thinking. He doesn't want your silence or your solutions. He just longs for an honest relationship. Tell Him the truth and ask for His help.

When we keep strong lines of communication with God, He hears us. He comes near. He sends His Holy Spirit to comfort us and give us wisdom. And He has a way of turning even the pittiest of circumstances into something beautiful.

I'm in the pits, Lord. I need You to rescue me. I don't know what You're doing, and I don't like it. But I trust You.

I know I'm worthy because He rescues me when I call.

Showing Up Tomorrow

So faith comes from hearing, and hearing through the word of Christ.
ROMANS 10:17 ESV

• •

Do you ever struggle with faith? That's normal. We all struggle sometimes. But when it's hard to keep moving forward in faith, it can be helpful to think about the meaning of the word. In simple terms, "faith" means showing up tomorrow. And the day after that. And the day after that.

So how do we build the strength and consistency to keep showing up for God, even when we don't feel like it? Even when it doesn't make sense? This verse gives us the answer—the recipe for faith.

Faith comes by hearing—or by reading and listening to what God has to say. We "hear" when we seek Him. We "hear" when we spend time with Him. The more time we spend with a person, the better we know them. Our relationship with God is no different.

When we truly, intimately know a person, we can trust what we know about their character. And when we truly, intimately know God, we know that above all, He is love. Consistent, passionate, powerful love, poured out on our behalf. His love for us does not change. The more we know that, the easier it is to have faith. To show up tomorrow—because we know He will do what He says.

Father, build my faith. Remind me to seek You and spend time with You, so I'll have the strength and consistency to show up tomorrow.

I know I'm worthy because my journey of
faith lights a path for my children's journeys.

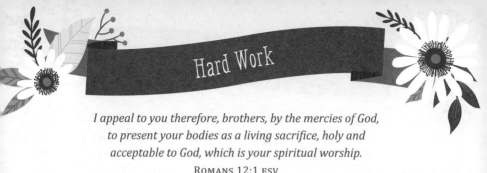

Hard Work

*I appeal to you therefore, brothers, by the mercies of God,
to present your bodies as a living sacrifice, holy and
acceptable to God, which is your spiritual worship.*
ROMANS 12:1 ESV

• •

In theory and in greeting cards, motherhood is all cuddles and hugs and soft, warm fuzzies floating like clouds, landing gently on our children's souls. In reality, motherhood involves sweat, sleepless nights, and hard physical labor. We stay awake with them when they're sick. We get up early, when our bodies scream for rest, to take them to band practice. We stay up late doing laundry because there's a soccer game tomorrow and we just pulled the uniform out from under the bed.

In so many ways, motherhood is hard.

But God sees. He knows what we go through. And somehow, in the mysterious way God has, He blends the physical with the spiritual. When our sacrifice for others leaves us bone weary, God counts it as righteousness. When we do things out of love, and we exhaust ourselves in the process, God credits it to our ledger. He carries us when we can't go on, and He marks it down in his memory bank: "Remember to bless her. She's gone above and beyond."

*I am worn out, Father. I want to bless my family, but some days
I feel like I can't take another step. Please give me rest that
only You can give. Accept my labor as a worship offering.*

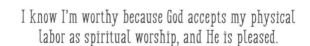

I know I'm worthy because God accepts my physical
labor as spiritual worship, and He is pleased.

Opportunities

Do not be conformed to this world, but be transformed by the renewal of your mind, that by testing you may discern what is the will of God, what is good and acceptable and perfect.
ROMANS 12:2 ESV

• •

In school, most of us dreaded test days. If we felt prepared, we might finish the test with a sense of victory. If we didn't study, it could ruin our day—not to mention our GPAs. Either way, a test was usually a pretty big deal.

But tests aren't just for the schoolroom. We learn God's will by testing. Instead of the word "test," it's helpful to think of it as an *opportunity* to show what we've learned or to understand His will. We can prepare for these "opportunities" by daily renewing our minds through prayer, worship, and reading His Word.

Are you going through a time of testing? Praise God! He's giving you a unique chance to know Him more and to understand His will. And the good news is, He is a kind and compassionate teacher. He wants us to win at life, and He cheers us on, gently guiding us on the right path and giving us the wisdom we need for each new opportunity.

I feel like I've failed lots of tests, Lord. But I'm grateful for each opportunity to know You more, to understand Your will, and to become like You.

I am worthy because God patiently works
with me as I become more like Him.

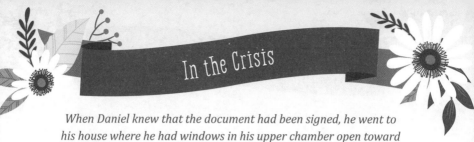

When Daniel knew that the document had been signed, he went to his house where he had windows in his upper chamber open toward Jerusalem. He got down on his knees three times a day and prayed and gave thanks before his God, as he had done previously.

DANIEL 6:10 ESV

• •

Daniel was faced with a serious dilemma. Some of his adversaries had convinced the king to sign papers forbidding anyone to pray to anyone other than King Darius for thirty days. Daniel could obey the decree and disobey God, or he could obey God and risk his own life. Though few of us will face death for our beliefs, most of us have experienced situations in which living out our faith wasn't popular.

We might call this a crisis of faith. When dealing with such a crisis, we can do what Daniel did: practice faith in the middle of the storm, knowing God will not forsake us. Remember, faith makes all things *possible* (Luke 1:37). It doesn't always make things *easy*.

God delivered Daniel from death, but He didn't take the trial away. Daniel had to face punishment and the possibility of death, not knowing what the outcome would be. Like Daniel, we can trust God. We can obey Him. And we can know that He will see us through the trial, with victory on the other side.

Help me remain faithful, even when obeying You isn't popular with those around me.

I know I'm worthy because God sees my faithful obedience. He will carry me through difficult times and show me victory on the other side.

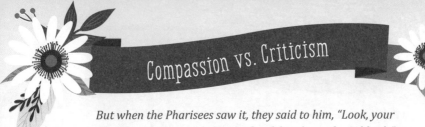

Compassion vs. Criticism

But when the Pharisees saw it, they said to him, "Look, your disciples are doing what is not lawful to do on the Sabbath."
MATTHEW 12:2 ESV

. . . .

Jesus and His disciples had preached to crowds, healed the sick, fed the hungry. . . and they were exhausted. So as they passed through some fields, they took a few handfuls of grain as a snack. That's when the Pharisees jumped in with an attack.

There was a law that said they couldn't do work on the Sabbath. Since harvesting grain was technically *work*, the Pharisees jumped at this "gotcha" moment. They were looking for something to accuse Jesus of.

It's important to remember that *Satan* is known as the accuser. He looks for things to criticize. He waits for the chance to catch us doing something wrong, and then he reminds us over and over of our failures.

God, on the other hand, is gracious and kind, patient and forgiving. He doesn't accuse us of sins we've already been forgiven for. He looks at our hearts more than He looks at our actions. If we mess up, but our hearts are right, He takes that into account.

When dealing with others, are we critical? Are we quick to accuse others, or do we show kindness, patience, and grace? When we align ourselves with God's values by acting with compassion and love, we show the people around us what God's love looks like.

Forgive me for being critical and quick to accuse.
Help me be kind and compassionate, like You.

I know I'm worthy because I model God's love for my family.

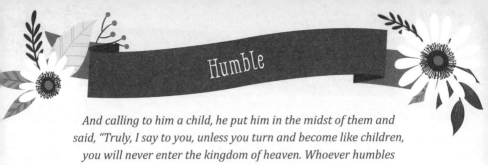

Humble

And calling to him a child, he put him in the midst of them and said, "Truly, I say to you, unless you turn and become like children, you will never enter the kingdom of heaven. Whoever humbles himself like this child is the greatest in the kingdom of heaven."

MATTHEW 18:2–4 ESV

Our culture has taken the word *pride* and made it a good thing. While there's nothing wrong with feeling good about our accomplishments and decisions, it's important to remember that pride is in direct opposition to what God wants from us. Humility, like that of a child, is what He desires.

A small child is totally dependent on the parent for everything. A good parent will provide for that child's needs, not because he's done anything to deserve it but because of love. When we feel like we're strong enough on our own, like we can handle things, like we can take care of everything by ourselves, that's pride. When we think we're always right and we know more than others, that's pride. When we refuse to yield. . .yeah, that's pride.

God is a good and loving Father. He provides everything we need. He wants us to trust Him, knowing He's got everything under control. It takes humility to yield our desires to God. But humility is exactly what He wants from us. When we humble ourselves, He is pleased, and He will do great things in our lives.

Father, I want to be humble. Make my heart like a little child's. I trust You completely.

I know I'm worthy because God is pleased with my humility.

No Freak-Out Needed

For God did not give us a spirit of timidity or cowardice or fear, but [He has given us a spirit] of power and of love and of sound judgment and personal discipline [abilities that result in a calm, well-balanced mind and self-control].
2 TIMOTHY 1:7 AMP

There's probably not a mom alive who hasn't had an occasional freak-out moment. We're late, and our child can't find a pair of matching shoes. Or we're told, on the way to school, that our child volunteered us to make cupcakes for the school bake sale, which is today. Or we find out our child's being bullied, and we don't know what to do.

When faced with these—and even tougher—situations, it's possible to remain calm. (Not easy, mind you. But it is possible.) God has given us everything we need to accomplish everything He wants us to accomplish. And since the most important priority on God's list is love, He will provide the calm, sound judgment to keep us from freaking out and will help us act with patience, kindness, and amazing problem-solving skills. No anxiety or fear, no freak-outs required.

I have far too many moments when I lose it, Lord. Stress builds up, surprises come my way, and I explode in a puddle of negative emotion. Thank You for this reminder that I can trust You to give me confidence, discipline, and calm self-control.

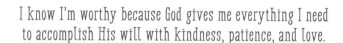

I know I'm worthy because God gives me everything I need
to accomplish His will with kindness, patience, and love.

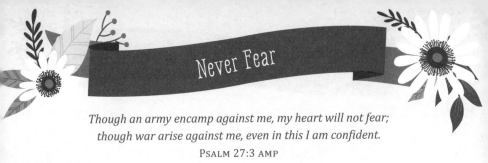

Never Fear

Though an army encamp against me, my heart will not fear;
though war arise against me, even in this I am confident.
PSALM 27:3 AMP

This life can present scary, bigger-than-our-nightmares situations. When those circumstances show up, our first, most natural response is fear. Sometimes, as in the case of those in the military, we might face a literal army encamped against us. Other times, we might face an unwanted medical diagnosis, job loss, financial struggle, or failing marriage. When faced with insurmountable conditions, it's best to find a quiet place, take some deep breaths, and remember who is in charge.

The fear comes when we think *we're* in charge. When we believe we're the ones responsible for conquering that army, climbing that mountain, or healing that disease, we feel powerless. But when we truly know that God is in control, that He knew about these events before we did, and that He already has a plan to bring everything together for good, we can relax. We may not like the circumstances, and that's okay. But we don't have to be terrified by them. God is all-powerful. His plans for us are good. And He loves us more than life.

Too often, my first response to stress is fear. Thank You for this
reminder that You are in control, no matter how crazy things
get. I trust You and Your love for me and my family.

I know I'm worthy because God never ignores my problems. He takes care of every circumstance, even when I can't see a way out.

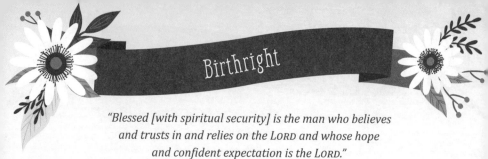

Birthright

*"Blessed [with spiritual security] is the man who believes
and trusts in and relies on the LORD and whose hope
and confident expectation is the LORD."*
JEREMIAH 17:7 AMP

When we were children in elementary school, we learned about antonyms. These words are opposites, like happy and sad, hot and cold, empty and full. But one pair of antonyms we may not have learned is *fear* and *hope*.

By definition, fear is the belief that something bad is about to happen. Hope is the belief that something good will happen. God has been very specific in His Word. Many times, He tells His children not to fear. Don't be afraid. Be strong and courageous. Time and again, He tells us to hope in Him, believe in Him, trust in Him. As His children, hope—confident expectation that good is in store—is our birthright.

Living in a perpetual state of fear and anxiety is not from God. When fear threatens to control us, we can tell Satan to shut up and leave us alone. We are royal daughters of the Most High God. He loves us, He has everything under control, and He has wonderful things in store for our lives.

*Lord, thank You for this reminder that fear is not from
You, but hope is. Remind me of who I am. Remind me
that hope is my birthright. I trust You completely.*

I know I'm worthy because I am a royal daughter of
the King of kings, and He loves me beyond measure.

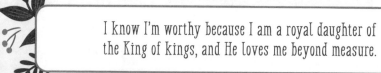

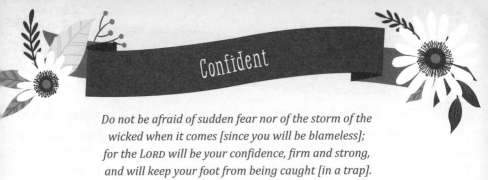

Confident

*Do not be afraid of sudden fear nor of the storm of the
wicked when it comes [since you will be blameless];
for the LORD will be your confidence, firm and strong,
and will keep your foot from being caught [in a trap].*
PROVERBS 3:25–26 AMP

• •

God's promises are for His children. He knows us better than anyone. He knows our faults, flaws, and foibles. He knows we'll mess up. Our mistakes don't negate His promises to us. He sees our hearts and our sincere desire to honor Him.

Those who don't try to please Him, those who live however they want, then try to claim His promises when it's convenient—those aren't the people this verse is speaking to. God's children—those whose lives show a consistent effort to obey Him—can have confidence in the face of any storm. He has our backs—and our fronts and our sides.

If you haven't been living for Him, it's never too late. God is gracious, and He longs for every person He created to be a part of His family. Choose Him now and move forward with confidence that you belong to Him. Leave fear in the past, and step into the future with strength, certainty, and hope in good things to come.

*Thank You for being my confidence, Lord. I know
You will take care of Your children, no matter what.*

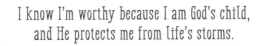

I know I'm worthy because I am God's child,
and He protects me from life's storms.

This is in accordance with [the terms of] the eternal purpose which He carried out in Christ Jesus our Lord, in whom we have boldness and confident access through faith in Him [that is, our faith gives us sufficient courage to freely and openly approach God through Christ].
EPHESIANS 3:11–12 AMP

In his letter to the church at Ephesus, Paul instructs the reader on two incredible benefits that come with being a Christian. The first is boldness. In this context, boldness refers to confidence, freedom, openness, and clarity. The boldness he refers to is for a specific purpose: to share Christ and to bring glory to God. When it comes to doing what we know God wants us to do, we can be bold and confident. We can speak freely about Him in order to draw attention to His love.

The next thing Paul points out is this idea of "confident access." Just ordinary people don't have unlimited access to the king of Spain or the US president. But the children of those high officials can talk to their parent any time they wish. We are God's children, and we can talk to God about anything we want, anytime we want.

The Christian life isn't always the easiest one, but the benefits package is excellent.

Thank You for giving me boldness to share my faith, and for giving me confident access to Your presence, any time I want.

I know I'm worthy because God gives me boldness and confident access.

His Grace Is Sufficient

But He has said to me, "My grace is sufficient for you [My lovingkindness and My mercy are more than enough—always available—regardless of the situation]; for [My] power is being perfected [and is completed and shows itself most effectively] in [your] weakness." Therefore, I will all the more gladly boast in my weaknesses, so that the power of Christ [may completely enfold me and] may dwell in me.
2 CORINTHIANS 12:9 AMP

When Paul wrote this, he'd been through some tough times. And scripture tells us he had a "thorn in the flesh," something ongoing that caused him a lot of pain. We're not sure if this "thorn" was physical, emotional, financial. . . . We just don't know. Whatever it was, Paul knew it kept him humble. It kept him fully dependent on God. And he knew God would always give him what he needed to keep going, for as long as God kept him on this earth.

The word *sufficient* in this passage is from the Greek *arkeo,* which means strength, endurance, and satisfaction. In other words, God's grace makes us strong enough. It helps us keep going. And when we fully lean into it, it helps us be content with our circumstances. When you face ongoing trials, and you wonder why God doesn't "fix" things, lean into Him. His power is on full display in our weakness.

I need Your grace, Father. Help me tap into the
strength and endurance You promised here.

I know I'm worthy because I don't have to be strong.
God wants to show off through my weakness.

91

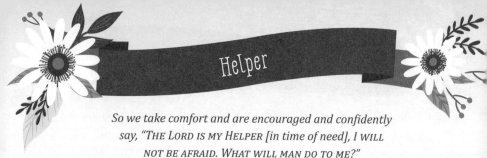

Helper

So we take comfort and are encouraged and confidently say, "THE LORD IS MY HELPER [in time of need], I WILL NOT BE AFRAID. WHAT WILL MAN DO TO ME?"
HEBREWS 13:6 AMP

• •

Imagine being the scrawny kid on the playground, and the bully decides to pick on you. He's tough. He's mean. And he wants to make an example of you in front of all the other kids. You look around for help, but everyone just backs away. You're on your own.

Now imagine your dad is a prize-winning bodybuilder. You sense, more than see, a presence behind you. A hulking shadow appears, covering both you and the bully. Suddenly the bully doesn't seem so big anymore. Suddenly he backs away, eyes wide, hands up. With a muscleman as your dad, what can that bully do to you?

Nothing. That's what.

Sometimes we forget who our Father is. He's beyond a muscleman. He's the King of kings. The Lord of lords. The Creator of the universe. His strength is unmatched, His power unrivaled. When hard times show up, taunting you, riling your fears, just take a deep breath and wait. Before long you'll sense His mighty presence over you. With Him on your side, nothing can stand against you.

When circumstances make me afraid for myself or my family, remind me of who You are. Let me feel Your presence.

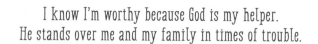

I know I'm worthy because God is my helper.
He stands over me and my family in times of trouble.

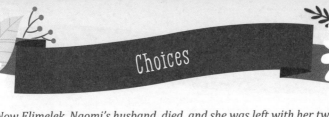

Choices

Now Elimelek, Naomi's husband, died, and she was left with her two sons. They married Moabite women, one named Orpah and the other Ruth. After they had lived there about ten years, both Mahlon and Kilion also died, and Naomi was left without her two sons and her husband.

RUTH 1:3–5 NIV

• •

Elimelek took his family and left Judah during a time of famine. They moved to Moab, a place God had denounced as being an evil city. Elimelek left God's chosen place and went somewhere God had warned against, because it seemed to have more to offer at the time. Perhaps it's not Elimelek's fault that he died, but now his wife and sons were stranded in a godforsaken place. Bad things always seem to happen when we step outside God's perfect plan for our lives.

Naomi's sons married local girls—who worshipped the local gods. Then the sons died, and Naomi was left with these two pagan daughters-in-law, in a time and place where women had few rights. That's how sin works—we take one step, just as Elimelek did. Then the second step is easier, and the third and fourth, until we find ourselves far from God's will. In this moment, Naomi had a choice. She could stay where she was, or she could go home. No matter our circumstances or whose fault they may be, we can always turn around. We can always go back to God's perfect will.

I'm sorry for the choices that have taken me out of Your perfect will. I want to come home.

I know I'm worthy because my choices can help lead my children toward God's perfect will.

Start Walking

When Naomi heard in Moab that the LORD had come to the aid of his people by providing food for them, she and her daughters-in-law prepared to return home from there. With her two daughters-in-law she left the place where she had been living and set out on the road that would take them back to the land of Judah.

RUTH 1:6–7 NIV

• •

Naomi was an impressive woman. She was a widow in a foreign land with a couple of widowed daughters-in-law in tow. In a country where Jewish people were hated, during a time when women were second-class citizens, with no trains, planes, or automobiles, and not even any comfort-sole sneakers, she decided to walk home.

And home was a long way away.

But she'd heard there was food back in Judah. Her family was there. She had friends and love and support there. She could have chosen to just stay put and live out her days in regret, but she didn't. When she found herself in a lousy circumstance, she decided to do something to change her situation.

Naomi had lived away from God long enough. She knew life was better within her Father's borders, so she strapped on her sandals and started walking. When we find ourselves far from God's perfect plan for our lives, we can do what Naomi did. Going back to where God is will make things better for ourselves, our children, and our entire families.

Lord, I want to be where You are. Show me the way.

I know I'm worthy because my decisions
can lead my family back to God.

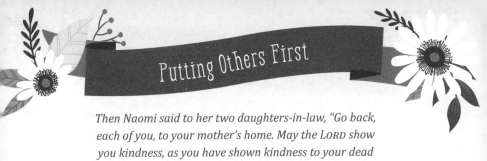

Putting Others First

Then Naomi said to her two daughters-in-law, "Go back, each of you, to your mother's home. May the LORD show you kindness, as you have shown kindness to your dead husbands and to me. May the LORD grant that each of you will find rest in the home of another husband."

RUTH 1:8–9 NIV

Naomi didn't have any daughters. These women were her daughters-in-law, her last connection to her deceased sons. Though they didn't share her faith in God, they were companions—women in a houseful of men. She didn't *want* to send them away, but she knew their lives would be better, or at least easier, if they stayed behind. She set her own feelings aside and encouraged them to do what was best for them.

That's what mothers do, isn't it? Putting others first doesn't come easily or naturally for anyone, yet that's one of the first steps in developing godly character. Truly, it's where real peace and happiness begin. When we live for ourselves, our capacity for joy is limited. But when we pour ourselves out for others, our ability to love grows, and joy comes back to us many times over.

Naomi was a wise woman. With God's help, that same selfless wisdom can live inside each of us.

Give me wisdom and humility, Lord, as I put others' needs before my own.

I am worthy because my choice to put others first
allows more room for love and joy in my life.

95

Stay Close

So Boaz said to Ruth, "My daughter, listen to me. Don't go and glean in another field and don't go away from here. Stay here with the women who work for me. Watch the field where the men are harvesting, and follow along after the women. I have told the men not to lay a hand on you. And whenever you are thirsty, go and get a drink from the water jars the men have filled."

RUTH 2:8–9 NIV

Ruth followed Naomi back to her home country of Judah—where Ruth was a foreigner. She was a Moabitess, and Jewish people weren't fond of Moabites. She went each day to glean in the fields, as that was the only way she and Naomi would have food to eat.

In this passage, Boaz, the owner of the field, noticed Ruth. He told her to stay close to him. In those days, a woman alone was vulnerable. She was open to insults, ridicule, and physical harm. Though Ruth had done nothing to deserve Boaz's attention, he noticed her. He cared for her, and he wanted to protect her.

God feels the same way about us. He loves us, and He offers His care and protection. The only requirement is that we stay close to Him. "Don't go wandering off. Stay right here, close to Me."

Thank You for Your protection over me and my family.
When I'm tempted to wander off, remind me to stay close to You.

I am worthy because God notices me and He wants to take care of me.

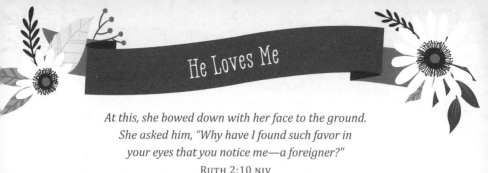

He Loves Me

At this, she bowed down with her face to the ground.
She asked him, "Why have I found such favor in
your eyes that you notice me—a foreigner?"
RUTH 2:10 NIV

• •

When Ruth followed Naomi back to Judah, she knew what she was in for. She was a foreigner in a strange land, an outcast. Perhaps she didn't own a mirror to see what Boaz saw, but it's clear she had *something* going for her. Boaz saw her and got hearts for eyes. He thought she was beautiful, and he fell in love.

Though Ruth may have been beautiful to Boaz, we don't have anything to offer God. We, more than Ruth, should fall on our faces and ask Him, "Why have I found such favor in Your eyes? Why have You noticed me?"

The answer to that question isn't found within us. We don't have to try to impress God; He's already noticed us. It's all about who He is. God loves us because He is love and it is His nature to love. He adores us with such passion that He gave His Son for us. We have favor with Him simply because He loves us, He loves us, He loves us! And nothing will ever separate us from His overwhelming love.

Thank You for noticing me, even when there's nothing much
to notice. Thank You for loving me and giving me worth.

I am worthy because God notices me, He values me,
and He loves me with all His heart.

Blessable

Boaz replied to her, "All that you have done for your mother-in-law after the death of your husband has been fully reported to me, and how you left your father and your mother and the land of your birth, and came to a people that you did not previously know. May the LORD reward your work, and may your wages be full from the LORD, the God of Israel, under whose wings you have come to take refuge."

RUTH 2:11–12 NASB

. . . .

We all want God's blessings, right? And we all have His blessings. He causes the rain to fall on dry ground. He sends sunshine and fields of flowers and children's laughter—it's all there for us to enjoy, whether we live for Him or not.

But God likes to cast extra portions of blessing on those who are *blessable*. He looks for consistent people—those who, over time, do their best to please Him. He's not impressed with occasional church attendance. He doesn't really care about single, grand gestures, like making a big donation to a good cause. Those are good things, but they're not what God wants most. What He wants most is our faithfulness. Our consistency.

He wants our hearts.

Boaz saw Ruth's consistency, and he admired her for it. He blessed her for it. In the same way, when our Father sees those faithful, day-by-day choices (the ones we think nobody notices), He blesses us.

Thank You for this reminder that You notice my faithfulness.
Help me remain steady, consistent, and blessable.

I am worthy because God notices my quiet
faithfulness, and He blesses me for it.

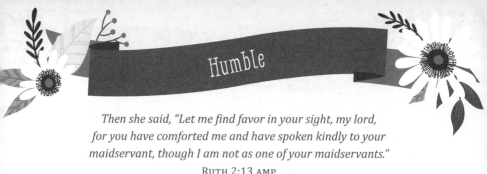

Humble

Then she said, "Let me find favor in your sight, my lord,
for you have comforted me and have spoken kindly to your
maidservant, though I am not as one of your maidservants."
RUTH 2:13 AMP

. . . .

The first thing Boaz noticed about Ruth was probably her physical beauty. But pretty faces aren't that uncommon. The next thing he noticed was something that made her even more beautiful—her humility. She was loyal to her mother-in-law. She worked hard, and she didn't expect special treatment from anyone. Instead, she was truly surprised when Boaz noticed her.

Humility is hard. It goes against our me-centered culture. We work hard so others will notice us. We give, expecting something back. We're kind to those who are kind to us. But God has called us to go against the grain of our human nature. He wants us to treat others like they're better than we are. He wants us to put others first, to defer to their needs, to honor them. This kind of humility is truly one of the best beauty treatments we can take part in. After all, isn't that what Christ did for us? And aren't we called to be like Him?

When we set aside our pride and act in humility, God notices. And He blesses us for it.

Help me set aside my pride and truly serve others with humility.
Show me how to do that in a way that honors You.

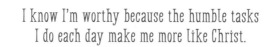

I know I'm worthy because the humble tasks
I do each day make me more like Christ.

Storybook Romance

At mealtime Boaz said to her, "Come over here and eat some bread and dip your bread in the vinegar." So she sat beside the reapers; and he served her roasted grain, and she ate until she was satisfied and she had some left [for Naomi].

RUTH 2:14 AMP

Boaz just met Ruth, and he's already asking her on a lunch date. Talk about love at first sight! He spared no effort to impress her; he served her from his own lunch and let her eat all she wanted.

Ruth's story may be a swoon-worthy romance, but you don't have to read her story to find that kind of love. You have a prince of your own—the Prince of Peace! He loves you with all His heart. He longs to spend each moment with you. He showers you with unexpected gifts, every single day. He loves you so much, He gave up heaven to rescue you. He gave His life to make you His own.

Ruth's story has a fairy-tale feel to it. She may have caught the eye of a wealthy landowner, but you've captured the love and attention of the King of kings. His love is more than a storybook romance. He wants you. He pursues you. And He rejoices when He knows He's captured your heart.

Thank You for loving me with a love that exceeds my imagination. I am Yours, Father—totally, completely Yours. My heart belongs to You.

> I know I'm worthy because the King of kings is in love with me.

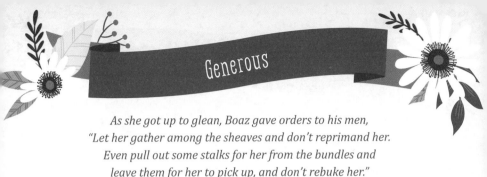

Generous

As she got up to glean, Boaz gave orders to his men,
"Let her gather among the sheaves and don't reprimand her.
Even pull out some stalks for her from the bundles and
leave them for her to pick up, and don't rebuke her."

RUTH 2:15–16 NIV

• •

Boaz was a generous man. He had no idea how this story would play out, but he knew Ruth and Naomi had a genuine need. It was common for landowners to leave some of their crops behind for the poor, but Boaz went beyond what was expected. He instructed his workers to be kind to Ruth. He even directed them to do some of the work for her and leave it where she could find it.

His generosity plays a leading role in this story. God uses Boaz's character as a reflection of His own generosity to us. And His ultimate goal is for us to become like Him. What would it take for us to go beyond what's expected? How can we make generosity a common practice in our family?

It starts with being generous with one another. Whether it's overlooking a failure or doing more than required, we can show our families what generosity looks like, right at home. And we can look for opportunities to be generous with others. We can donate sacrificially. We can give new things instead of just the leftovers. When we make generosity a standard, we teach God's character to our children.

Teach me to give—and to love—generously.

I know I'm worthy because my generosity reflects God's character.

Running Over

So Ruth gleaned in the field until evening. Then she threshed the barley she had gathered, and it amounted to about an ephah. She carried it back to town, and her mother-in-law saw how much she had gathered. Ruth also brought out and gave her what she had left over after she had eaten enough.

RUTH 2:17–18 NIV

Ruth stayed late and worked hard. It was sweaty, backbreaking labor. When evening came, she gathered as much barley as she could carry and took it home.

Naomi must have been overwhelmed, and maybe a little confused. How could one woman gather this much food? Where did she get this already-cooked meal? What was going on?

Ruth worked hard, and Naomi reaped the benefits. That's the way God works. When we live consistently for Him, when we try to please Him every single day, we're not the only ones who are blessed. Our families are also blessed because of our faithfulness.

We often look for ways to show our loved ones just how precious they are to us. We buy little gifts and cook special meals. But the best way we can show our families we love them is to live our lives in a way that honors God. When we do this, He pours His blessings into our lives until they're overflowing, running over onto the people we care about most.

I want to live for You so much that
Your presence spills onto my family.

I know I'm worthy because my choices bless my family.

Showing Off

Her mother-in-law asked her, "Where did you glean today? Where did you work? Blessed be the man who took notice of you!" Then Ruth told her mother-in-law about the one at whose place she had been working. "The name of the man I worked with today is Boaz," she said. "The Lord bless him!" Naomi said to her daughter-in-law. "He has not stopped showing his kindness to the living and the dead." She added, "That man is our close relative; he is one of our guardian-redeemers."

RUTH 2:19–20 NIV

· ·

In verse 18, we're told that Ruth gathered about an ephah, which is a Hebrew unit of dry measure equal to a bushel. According to some sources, that's around thirty-five liters. Have you ever tried carrying thirty-five liters of groceries by yourself? Ruth must have had some strong arms.

When Naomi saw all the barley, she didn't say, "Good job, Ruth. You've worked hard." She knew this was more than one woman could gather in a day. She knew someone had helped things along.

God works that way too. When we're doing all we can, when we're working hard and doing our best to please Him, He likes to show up and show off. He'll cause things to happen that are far beyond our ability, because He wants to get the credit.

Show off in my life, Lord. I want You to get all the glory.

> I know I'm worthy because my sincere efforts, paired with God's work in my life, cause great things to happen.

And Ruth the Moabite said, "Besides, he said to me, 'You shall keep close by my young men until they have finished all my harvest.' " And Naomi said to Ruth, her daughter-in-law, "It is good, my daughter, that you go out with his young women, lest in another field you be assaulted." So she kept close to the young women of Boaz, gleaning until the end of the barley and wheat harvests. And she lived with her mother-in-law.

RUTH 2:21–23 ESV

When Ruth followed Naomi to Bethlehem, she didn't have any grand illusions of an easy life. She was a foreigner, an outcast, and she expected to be treated as such. She'd already had her heart broken when her husband died. If she couldn't have him, she figured she'd at least stay with his mother. She had no reason to believe she'd find happiness again.

We all endure seasons of sadness. But God loves us, and He doesn't want us to live that way. With God, joy comes in the morning (Psalm 30:5)! When we go through a dark time, the most important thing we can do is stay close to God. He comforts. He heals. And if we follow Him, He will take us from a barren wasteland to a land flowing with milk and honey—or barley, as in Ruth's case.

Sometimes depression threatens to control me, Lord. Remind me to stay close to You. I need Your comfort and healing. I know You have good things in store for my life.

I know I'm worthy because I teach my children how to follow God even in difficult times.

Then Naomi her mother-in-law said to her, "My daughter, should I not seek rest for you, that it may be well with you? Is not Boaz our relative, with whose young women you were? See, he is winnowing barley tonight at the threshing floor. Wash therefore and anoint yourself, and put on your cloak and go down to the threshing floor, but do not make yourself known to the man until he has finished eating and drinking. But when he lies down, observe the place where he lies. Then go and uncover his feet and lie down, and he will tell you what to do." And she replied, "All that you say I will do."

RUTH 3:1–5 ESV

Ruth came from a pagan background. She had little hope of understanding Jewish laws and customs. But praise God, she had Naomi to help her. Naomi explained to Ruth exactly what she needed to do to let Boaz know she was interested. In a way, Naomi was both coach and cheerleader.

In this passage, Naomi paints a beautiful portrait of the Holy Spirit. As humans, our brains have trouble understanding God's ways. We don't know how to act like God's children. It doesn't come naturally to us. Just as Naomi acted as Ruth's cheerleader and guide, the Holy Spirit cheers us on. He shows us exactly what we need to know by giving us wisdom and understanding.

Thank You for Your Holy Spirit. Help me listen, trust, and obey.

I know I'm worthy because my sensitive obedience sets the tone for my family's attitude toward holy things.

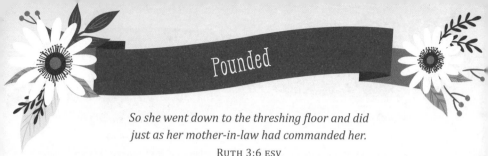

Pounded

So she went down to the threshing floor and did
just as her mother-in-law had commanded her.
RUTH 3:6 ESV

- -

Do you know what they do on the threshing floor?

They thresh things. They pound them repeatedly, to separate the good from the bad. They keep the wheat and throw out the weeds and other useless material. Another form of this word is "thrashing." Most of us know what it means to receive a thrashing.

A sane person would never choose a thrashing, but that's what life does to us sometimes. And while it's never a pleasant experience to be pounded, it's the threshing that gets rid of the bad stuff in our lives. It's the hard things that make us more like Him.

It seems crazy to say, "Go ahead, God! Pound me to a pulp. Beat the sin out of me. I can take it." But life's hardest circumstances often bring about the most growth and turn us into people who look more like our Father. Those seasons make us wiser, more loving, more forgiving, more compassionate. Those times make us gentler, kinder, more generous.

The thresher wouldn't waste time pounding something that had no value. In the same way, God lets us go through hard times because He sees our potential, and He wants to refine us.

This is a hard prayer, Lord. . . . But thank You for loving me enough
to let me be pounded. Do whatever it takes. I want to be like You.

I am worthy because God sees my value.

The Long Night

And when Boaz had eaten and drunk, and his heart was merry,
he went to lie down at the end of the heap of grain. Then she came
softly and uncovered his feet and lay down. At midnight the man was
startled and turned over, and behold, a woman lay at his feet!

RUTH 3:7–8 ESV

Naomi's instructions to lie down at Boaz's feet in the middle of the night probably seemed as strange to Ruth as they do to us. The threshing floor was a public place. Many of the workers slept there. She had to avoid waking anyone up.

When she finally found her place near Boaz, she probably didn't sleep a wink. She wondered how this plan would play out. Would he wake up? Would he notice her? Would he be angry she was there? That was surely one of the longest nights of Ruth's life.

We all have long nights when we can't sleep. We wonder what will happen next in our lives. We wonder if God sees us, if He notices what we're going through. We may even wonder if He's angry with us. But just as Boaz was in love with Ruth, God is in love with each of us.

He's already noticed you. He knows exactly what you're going through. And He promises to take care of you for the rest of your days.

I'm going through a long night right now, Lord. I know You see
me. I know You love me. Thank You for caring for all my needs.

I am worthy because God is in love with me.

Under His Wings

In the middle of the night something startled the man; he turned—
and there was a woman lying at his feet! "Who are you?" he asked.
"I am your servant Ruth," she said. "Spread the corner of your garment
over me, since you are a guardian-redeemer of our family."

RUTH 3:8–9 NIV

. . . .

When a mother hen has new chicks, they can disappear right into her feathers. She fluffs herself up, spreads her wings, and invites her babies to hide there. She protects them at night and keeps them warm in cool weather. As long as they're under her wings, they are secure.

In Hebrew, the corners of a garment were called wings. Ruth literally said, "Cover me with your wings. Take care of me and protect me." She humbly asked him to be her hero, her rescuer.

If a baby chick has an independent streak and chooses to run away from its mother, there's a good chance harm will come in the form of a hawk, a snake, or some other predator. Only by staying close can the young bird remain protected.

In the same way, God invites us to hide under His wings. He longs to cover us with His love. But if we choose not to stay close to Him, we forfeit the protection He provides. He longs to be our hero, our rescuer. But like Ruth, we must humble ourselves and remain near Him.

Spread Your wings over me and my family,
Father. We need Your protection.

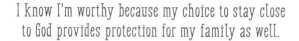

I know I'm worthy because my choice to stay close
to God provides protection for my family as well.

When Morning Comes

So she lay at his feet until morning, but got up before anyone could be recognized; and he said, "No one must know that a woman came to the threshing floor." He also said, "Bring me the shawl you are wearing and hold it out." When she did so, he poured into it six measures of barley and placed the bundle on her. Then he went back to town.

RUTH 3:14–15 NIV

The next morning, Boaz wanted to make sure Ruth wasn't the subject of cruel gossip. He sent her away early, but he didn't send her away empty handed. He gave her more than twice the amount of barley he'd given her on the day they met. He wanted to be sure she understood his commitment to her. It's as if he said, "Don't worry. You're mine, and I'm going to take care of you. Here's a little gift, just so you know how serious I am."

You may be going through a long night right now. You may feel like you're taking a pounding. Hang in there, because morning is on its way. God is committed to you. Often, after we go through a difficult time, God makes Himself known to us. He pours out His Spirit on us. He drenches us with His love, His blessings, His generosity. He wants us to know He's serious about His promise never to leave us or forsake us.

Hold on. Before you know it, morning will come.

It's been a long night, Lord, but I know You love me. I trust Your goodness and generosity. Thank You for the blessings I know You have in store for me and my family.

I am worthy because I'm the recipient of God's love and generosity.

When Ruth came to her mother-in-law, Naomi asked, "How did it go, my daughter?" Then she told her everything Boaz had done for her and added, "He gave me these six measures of barley, saying, 'Don't go back to your mother-in-law empty-handed.' "

RUTH 3:16–17 NIV

• •

This had been a long night for Naomi as well as for Ruth. After all, Naomi had no heirs, no one to take care of her. If Ruth married Boaz and had a son, Naomi's deceased husband's land would pass to that child. Naomi's place in the family would be secure.

Ruth and Naomi had lots of girl talk to catch up on. Then, Ruth said, "Oh! I almost forgot. Boaz sent this for you."

This is where we need to rewind to Ruth 1:21 (NIV), where a bitter Naomi said, "I went away full, but the LORD has brought me back empty." Now, in Ruth 3:17, Naomi is given enough groceries to last a good while.

Rewind and fast forward to those two scriptures until it sinks in. Naomi left God's promised land full but returned empty. Now she was back in the promised land, and she was full again. It's never God that leaves us wanting. It's the world that does that.

When you feel empty, hollow, sucked dry, go sit at your Father's feet and wait. Cling to Him. He wants to fill You up with His peace, His mercy, His love, and the riches of His blessings.

Forgive me for blaming You for the emptiness in my life. Fill me up, Lord.

I am worthy because God longs to fill me with His goodness.

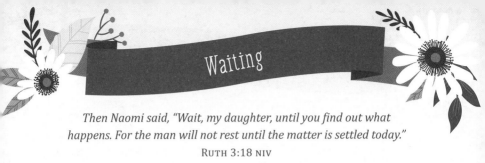

Waiting

Then Naomi said, "Wait, my daughter, until you find out what happens. For the man will not rest until the matter is settled today."
RUTH 3:18 NIV

Have you ever watched expectant grandparents in a hospital, waiting for their grandchild to be born? They pace. They fret. They check the clock and their watches, and they drive the poor hospital attendant crazy, asking for updates. Yet all their fretting and pacing will do nothing to influence the course of events. They're better off sitting down, putting their feet up, and reading a good book.

Sometimes we feel something big is about to happen, and we want to hurry things along. We're tempted to worry and fret and manipulate things to our advantage. But many times, the thing God wants us to do most of all is *wait*. No amount of nail-biting or chocolate consumption will change the outcome, but we can breathe easy, knowing God has it all under control.

In Psalms, David wrote, "I remain confident of this: I will see the goodness of the LORD in the land of the living. Wait for the LORD; be strong and take heart and wait for the LORD" (Psalm 27:13–14 NIV). Waiting requires trust. It requires faith in God's goodness. Just as Naomi had confidence that Boaz would take care of things, we can relax, knowing God, who never sleeps, is working on our behalf.

Thank You for working for my cause, Father.
Help me rest in You. I trust Your goodness.

I am worthy because God is working all things together for my good.

Meanwhile Boaz went up to the town gate and sat down there just as the guardian-redeemer he had mentioned came along. Boaz said, "Come over here, my friend, and sit down." So he went over and sat down. Boaz took ten of the elders of the town and said, "Sit here," and they did so.
RUTH 4:1–2 NIV

In Jewish culture, the closest male relative of a deceased man had the right to claim that man's property. But if he did so, he also had to take care of that man's family. In this case, he'd have to marry Ruth and take care of Naomi. Boaz loved Ruth, but he was only the *second* closest relative. He needed to go about things the right way if he wanted to claim Ruth as his own. So he went to the place where everyone was bound to show up at some point—the town gate.

He could have just eloped. But then Ruth would have never truly been accepted as a respectable woman. Boaz wanted better for Ruth, so much so that he'd rather risk losing her to this other man than put her through a lifetime of shame.

Sometimes we're tempted to take shortcuts to make things happen faster or to manipulate the outcome. But God wants us to be above reproach, or blameless. When we do things the right way, we model good character for our children, and we invite God's blessings.

Help me do things the right way, even when it's hard.

I know I'm worthy because my actions teach my children about good character.

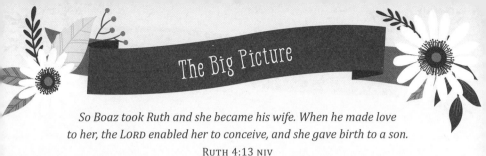

The Big Picture

So Boaz took Ruth and she became his wife. When he made love to her, the LORD enabled her to conceive, and she gave birth to a son.
RUTH 4:13 NIV

• •

In many ways, Ruth had a hard life. She was a young widow. She left her home to go to a foreign land where, because of her race, she was despised. She had to work hard for every meal. And yet, each step of the way, God had a plan. His hand was on Ruth's life, because He had something bigger in store than she could have imagined.

The child born to Boaz and Ruth became the grandfather of King David. And later, following the same lineage, came Jesus. God used Ruth, a foreigner, an outcast, to graft the Gentiles into the line of Christ.

God's plans for our lives are always bigger than our own plans. He often doesn't share those plans with us because we'd be overwhelmed. We might even try to hurry things along and mess everything up in the process. He is God, and He is under no obligation to let us in on what He's doing. But we can trust that yes, He is working.

Though we only see what's right in front of us, God sees the bigger picture, and He's orchestrating everything to turn out for our good and His glory.

Help me trust You even when I don't know what You're doing.

I know I'm worthy because I am part of God's big picture.

Unashamed

As far as the east is from the west, so far does he remove our transgressions from us. As a father shows compassion to his children, so the LORD shows compassion to those who fear him.
PSALM 103:12–13 ESV

We all have things we're ashamed of. But God doesn't want us to feel ashamed. Psalm 3:3 says He's the lifter of our heads. He hates our sin, but He loves *us*. When He knows how very sorry we are that we messed up, He flexes His mighty muscle. He takes our mistakes and our mishaps and even our rebellion, balls it up, and casts it as far from us as it can go: as far as the east is from the west. In other words, He gets rid of it completely, because He doesn't want it defining us.

But we have an accuser: Satan. And Satan wants us to feel ashamed. If he can keep us bogged down in the past, living in regret, feeling like failures, he wins. That's how he destroys us.

God will win the war against Satan. But when it comes to who wins the everyday battles, a lot of that depends on us. It depends on who we listen to, who we believe. We can listen to Satan and walk around, heads hung, living in shame. Or we can believe God when He tells us we belong to Him, that we're daughters of the King of kings. And there's certainly no shame in that.

Thank You for lifting my head. Remind me to listen only to You.

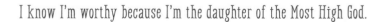

I know I'm worthy because I'm the daughter of the Most High God.

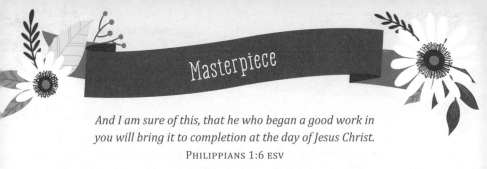

Masterpiece

And I am sure of this, that he who began a good work in you will bring it to completion at the day of Jesus Christ.
PHILIPPIANS 1:6 ESV

• •

Do you ever get impatient with God? Most of us wish He'd just go ahead and do what He's going to do. Doesn't He have a blueprint to follow? What takes Him so long?

But God has all the time in the world. He's in no hurry. Rather than just slapping together a substandard version of our souls, He likes to take his time, sculpting us into a beautiful masterpiece.

He's not a quitter either. He began His work in us on the day of our conception. From the moment we had life, He began drawing us to Himself, longing for us to someday choose a relationship with Him. And He's been whittling away at our souls since long before we knew He existed. He's molding, sculpting, carving. . . discarding the needless, ugly, useless parts, leaving behind only what is lovely and true and perfect. And He takes His time doing it because He already knows the finished product, and He wants it to be just right.

God is the master architect, and He holds the blueprints of our lives. Trust Him. He will not leave His work undone. Let Him have His way, and the final results will be stunningly, breathtakingly beautiful.

Thank You for making my life into a masterpiece.
Give me patience as I wait for the final product.

I am worthy because God is making something beautiful of my life.

Now and Then

Yes, and I will rejoice, for I know that through your prayers and the help of the Spirit of Jesus Christ this will turn out for my deliverance, as it is my eager expectation and hope that I will not be at all ashamed, but that with full courage now as always Christ will be honored in my body, whether by life or by death. For to me to live is Christ, and to die is gain.
PHILIPPIANS 1:18–21 ESV

• •

Wow. Paul was imprisoned, awaiting trial. He knew that one of two things would happen: he'd be set free, or he'd be executed. Yet he was able to find good in either outcome! If he lived, he'd keep pursuing his passionate goal of sharing Christ. If he died, he'd *be* with Christ, face-to-face.

We can learn from Paul. We often view death as scary or sad. But for the Christian, death is a step up from this life. Sometimes we get depressed and we wish we could just "go home." But this life is filled with opportunities to serve Christ, who loves us so much that He gave His life for us. Like Paul, each day of our lives should be lived as a joyful *thank-you* to the one who gave us life. And like Paul, death, in its proper time, should be viewed as an exciting prospect to see Christ for all of eternity.

Thank You for Paul's brave example of faith and commitment. Help me to model my faith after his.

I know I'm worthy because God uses me to honor Christ.

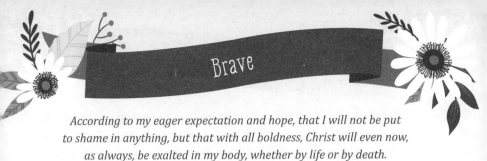

Brave

*According to my eager expectation and hope, that I will not be put
to shame in anything, but that with all boldness, Christ will even now,
as always, be exalted in my body, whether by life or by death.*

PHILIPPIANS 1:20 NASB

Paul was a hero of our faith. He was unshakable, unmovable—right? This verse shows us that Paul was human. He had fears and doubts, just like the rest of us.

Listen to him. *I sure hope I won't get cold feet. I hope I won't have a reason to be ashamed of myself. I hope Christ won't be ashamed of me! I must be brave. I know I can be brave!* His words above seem like a self-directed pep talk. He wants Christ to be exalted in his life and in his death. But he knows that things could get pretty scary at his upcoming trial.

Faith is hard sometimes. If it were easy, then we'd have many, many more committed Christians in this world. There's no shame in feeling afraid or having doubts. The shame comes only when, in our fear and doubt, we turn *away* from God instead of *to* Him. Like Paul, we can square our shoulders, lift our chins, and proceed into the uncertain future with determination to serve our Savior, no matter what.

*I admit that sometimes I feel afraid, Lord. Sometimes my faith
gets shaken. Please help me during those times to cling to You.*

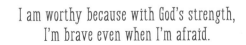

I am worthy because with God's strength,
I'm brave even when I'm afraid.

Mission Statement

But if I am to live on in the flesh, this will mean fruitful labor for me; and I do not know which to choose. But I am hard-pressed from both directions, having the desire to depart and be with Christ, for that is very much better; yet to remain on in the flesh is more necessary for your sakes.

PHILIPPIANS 1:22–24 NASB

Paul had a clearly defined goal and purpose for living. He had a mission. That mission was his motivation to keep going. His goal was to share the good news of Jesus Christ with everyone. Period.

It's easy to drift through life without a clearly defined reason for living. We have fuzzy ambitions, hazy aspirations. Yet each of us needs a purpose, or we'll feel useless and unappreciated. Without a clear cause, without a definite motivation for life, we can get depressed and disheartened.

It's important to have a mission statement. Whether we write it out or simply paste it onto our mental files, we need to establish our main purpose for living. Then, from time to time, we can evaluate our lives and see how we're coming along. Paul knew his mission was still being accomplished, and it gave him a reason to keep going. What is your mission? Are you headed in the right direction? If not, what do you need to do to change directions?

Thank You for placing in me the desire for a purpose. Please let my goals and ambitions honor You, and help me accomplish them.

I know I'm worthy because my mission
and purpose for this life are important.

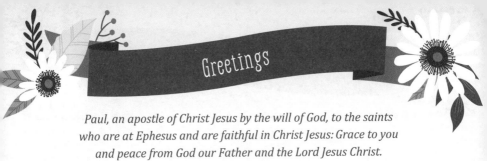

Greetings

Paul, an apostle of Christ Jesus by the will of God, to the saints who are at Ephesus and are faithful in Christ Jesus: Grace to you and peace from God our Father and the Lord Jesus Christ.

<small>EPHESIANS 1:1–2 NASB</small>

· ·

Paul opens this letter, *Grace and peace to you. . . .* Just pretty words of greeting? Hardly. To truly appreciate this greeting, we must understand a little about the words *grace* and *peace*.

The Greek word for *grace* is *charis*. *Grace* means something wonderful that is given as a gift. It's something totally undeserved that brings great joy. The Greek word for *joy* is *chara*, so you can see how closely the two are related.

The meaning used here for *peace* comes from the Hebrew word *shalom*. In western culture, we tend to think of *peace* as *the absence of war.* In this context, peace didn't refer to the absence of something as much as it referred to the presence of someone—the glorious, bountiful, blessed presence of God. For of course, where God is, there is peace. A lack of peace often comes from the absence of God in our lives.

Paul wishes each and every one of us *charis* and *shalom.* We can be certain that God longs for each of us to experience His amazing, wonderful presence, along with the beautiful, bountiful, joy-producing gifts that come only from Him.

Thank You for the grace and peace that come
from having a right relationship with You.

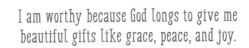

I am worthy because God longs to give me
beautiful gifts like grace, peace, and joy.

Good Gifts

Blessed be the God and Father of our Lord Jesus Christ, who has blessed us with every spiritual blessing in the heavenly places in Christ.
EPHESIANS 1:3 NASB

It's fun to imagine what heaven will be like. Chocolate has to be included—and cheesecake. Best of all, calories will be a thing of the past.

All kidding aside, heaven will be wonderful simply because God is there. Jesus will be the only light we need. Every good and perfect gift—love, joy, peace, patience, kindness, goodness, self-control, humility, forgiveness. . .these are just a few things we struggle with here but will have in abundance in heaven.

We don't have to wait until heaven to experience these *heavenly* gifts! God's given us all we need, right here and now, to have these qualities in our lives. They are heavenly because they are eternal, unlike the earthly gifts of wealth or physical beauty or temporary fame.

When Paul wrote these words, he was destitute. He didn't have many earthly blessings, yet he considered himself rich. God had provided him with everything he needed to live a joyful, peaceful, abundant life.

We often attach the word "blessings" to temporary gifts. We're blessed with houses, cars, jobs, good health, and plenty to eat. But those blessings won't last. As children of the Most High King, we've been given gifts that will truly provide us with "the good life"—both now and for eternity.

Thank You for giving me everything I need to live a joyous, peaceful, rewarding life in You.

I am worthy because God gives me amazing gifts I can use right now.

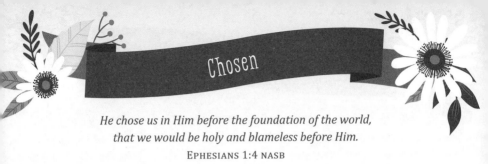

Chosen

He chose us in Him before the foundation of the world,
that we would be holy and blameless before Him.
EPHESIANS 1:4 NASB

· ·

Do you remember that feeling, in third grade, when the teacher lined everyone up, appointed team captains, and told them to choose teams? I hated those times. My palms got all sweaty. I could barely breathe. *Pick me, pick me, please pick me.* If the teams were athletic, I was often the last picked. But if they were choosing for the spelling bee, I was first choice.

It feels good to be chosen.

Guess what? We have already been *chosen.* The King of kings chose each one of us before time began. He thought us up, called us by name, and chose us for His own.

He wants us.

But here's something even more amazing: the God of the universe chose to humble Himself. He put Himself in the line, so to speak, and He wants *us* to choose *Him.* He sits on His throne in heaven whispering *Pick Me, pick Me, please pick Me....*

God could have created robots who have no choice but to love Him, but He didn't. He chose us, and now He stretches out His arm in a divine invitation to choose Him back. When we do, heaven rejoices. Then He begins His work in us, making us more like Him, creating in us a family resemblance of holiness and blamelessness so that all the world can see—we have been *chosen.*

Thank You for choosing me, Father. I choose You back.

I am worthy because God chose me.

Redeemed

In him we have redemption through his blood, the forgiveness of sins,
in accordance with the riches of God's grace that he lavished on us.
EPHESIANS 1:7–8 NIV

My grandmother used to shop at Brookshire Brothers, where she'd earn little green savings stamps. When she'd saved enough stamps, she could *redeem* them by trading them for dishes or bath towels or electric can openers.

That picture of the word *redeem* doesn't come close to describing the redemption Paul speaks of. In ancient wartime, when people were captured by the enemy, they were turned into slaves. But important people were sometimes worth more as moneymakers than laborers. So these officials and dignitaries, now slaves, could be *redeemed* at a high price.

We're slaves to sin. But there's good news: *we are important to God.* To Him, we're worth an extremely high price. God sent Christ to die because death was the price required to set us free. Now, because that price has been paid, we no longer have to be slaves. If we continue in slavery, it is because we choose to, not because we must.

But God didn't stop there. He has *lavished* His grace on us. *Lavished* describes going far beyond what's needed or expected. Think about that. *We were slaves. God paid the ultimate price for us. He set us free. Then He **lavished** His grace on us.*

That's the best rags-to-riches story I've ever heard.

Thank You for paying the ultimate price for
me and for lavishing Your grace on me.

I know I'm worthy because God paid a high price for me.

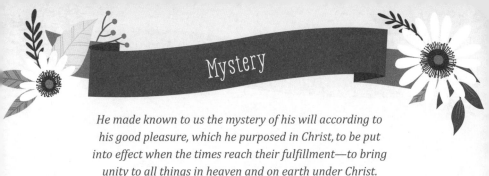

Mystery

He made known to us the mystery of his will according to his good pleasure, which he purposed in Christ, to be put into effect when the times reach their fulfillment—to bring unity to all things in heaven and on earth under Christ.

EPHESIANS 1:9–10 NIV

• •

During biblical times and throughout history, many religions emphasized *secrets.* There were secret rituals, secret sacrifices, secret writings.... People would have been familiar with the *mystery* of divine things.

But God has no desire to hide things from His children. He makes His love clear to us all. It's so easy that we often have a hard time understanding its simplicity. But God will reveal Himself to anyone who seeks Him. No mystery.

God's desire is that every person will be adopted into His family. To make that happen, He sent His Son. Jesus didn't act on His own but in accordance with His Father's purpose and plan. Christ died for us, and then He did what only God can do—He conquered death and rose again. He paid the price for us that no one else could pay.

We each have a choice. We can choose to accept what Christ did for us on the cross, or not. But one day—oh! That glorious day!—one day every creature on heaven and on earth and under the earth will bow down and recognize Christ for who He is: King of kings and Lord of lords.

Thank You for making Yourself known to me and for providing a way for me to become Your child.

I know I'm worthy because God lets me in on His secrets.

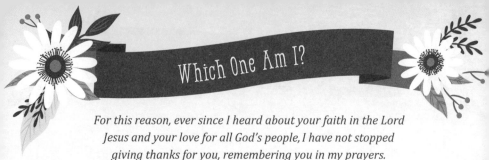

Which One Am I?

For this reason, ever since I heard about your faith in the Lord
Jesus and your love for all God's people, I have not stopped
giving thanks for you, remembering you in my prayers.
EPHESIANS 1:15–16 NIV

Have you noticed it's easy to be thankful for the faithful, loving people in your life? These are people who help when you're in trouble. They make you feel special and wanted and loved, so you try to return the favor. You love and pray for them because they're easy to love, easy to pray for.

Unfortunately, we have other people in our lives too. You know who I'm talking about. The ones who don't love you, or at least they don't show it well. Those who are unkind, gossipy, unreliable, and mean. These are the people who don't exhibit the lovely qualities that *should* be present in those who have placed their faith in Christ.

We should all ask ourselves: *Which list am I on? When people think of me, are they thankful? Or does my name bring a sense of dread?*

It should be our goal, as Christians, to display His love so boldly that every person we meet feels it. When others are around us, they should feel wanted. Loved. Needed. Special. After all, that is the way Christ feels about us. He loves us beyond measure, and He calls us to love others the way He loves us.

Help me exhibit faith and love so those around me will be drawn to YOU.

I know I'm worthy because my loving
words and actions draw people to Christ.

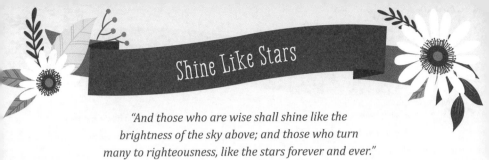

Shine Like Stars

*"And those who are wise shall shine like the
brightness of the sky above; and those who turn
many to righteousness, like the stars forever and ever."*
DANIEL 12:3 ESV

The book of Daniel is filled with weird visions about end-times. Even Daniel admits he didn't understand all of them. But toward the end of the book, this verse stands out like a beacon in the chaos. Its message is clear: those who seek God, who live by His wisdom, and who point others to Him will be rewarded.

Sometimes it can feel like our faithfulness and good deeds go unnoticed. Though the people around us may take us for granted, we can be certain that God notices. He cares. And He is already lining up our place of honor for all eternity. We will have our moment of glory. More than a moment, actually. We will shine like stars for all eternity.

So next time you feel like having a meltdown but wisdom keeps your emotions under control, remember that God notices. Next time you show kindness to someone who doesn't deserve it in order to reflect God's love, you can be certain God sees, and He is pleased. Those deeds will be rewarded.

*Lord, give me wisdom in those times when I don't know what to do
or how to respond. Help me reflect Your love and point others to You,
even when it's hard. More than anything, I want to please You.*

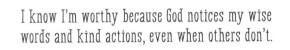

I know I'm worthy because God notices my wise
words and kind actions, even when others don't.

He Gets You

And wherever he came, in villages, cities, or countryside, they laid the sick in the marketplaces and implored him that they might touch even the fringe of his garment. And as many as touched it were made well.

MARK 6:56 ESV

You know that feeling you get when you're exhausted and the sink is piled with dishes and mounds of laundry are everywhere, and you can hardly tell which clothes are clean and which are dirty, and echoes of "*Mom, I'm hungry,*" and "*Honey, where are my car keys?*" fill every inch, every cranny of your house? Yeah. Jesus knew that feeling. Everywhere He went, somebody wanted a piece of Him.

He gets you. He understands. And His Holy Spirit stands nearby, cheering you on—because each time someone tugs on you, each time you fold that laundry or do those dishes or go to work when you're borderline sick so you can pay the bills. . .each of those are opportunities to show love. Jesus cared deeply about the people around Him, and so do you. When you act in love, even when it's hard, you're imitating Jesus.

I know You understand what it feels like to be exhausted, to want a little time for yourself, and to press on anyway because You care about the people around You. Give me Your strength, Lord. And when appropriate, give me some time to rest in You.

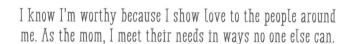

I know I'm worthy because I show love to the people around me. As the mom, I meet their needs in ways no one else can.

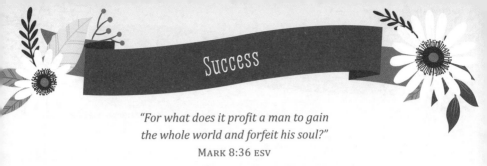

Success

*"For what does it profit a man to gain
the whole world and forfeit his soul?"*
MARK 8:36 ESV

· ·

When you were young, back when you still believed anything was possible, what were your dreams? What did you want to do and be when you grew up? Perhaps you had aspirations of becoming a professional ballerina or musician. Maybe you wanted to be a doctor or lawyer with your own practice. Maybe being a mom was your dream, but in those visions, you always had a clean house and perfectly behaved children.

There's nothing wrong with having goals. Even at this point, none of your God-given dreams are out of reach. But it's important to remember that your success doesn't rest on those dreams. Success by the world's standards looks like fame, fortune, and a fancy car. This kind of "success" is a lie designed to steal your soul, your years, your relationships, and your life.

Redefine your definition of success using God's dictionary. By His standards, success means loving Him with your whole heart. It means loving others and putting their needs before your own. It means being humble yet strong. It means being kind when being cruel comes more naturally. Though His definition of success may not be as glamorous, it's more real. It's more complete. True joy and fulfillment comes not through worldly success but through becoming like Him.

*Help me redefine my definition of success by
Your standards. I want to be just like You.*

I know I'm worthy because the love I show
others makes me successful in God's eyes.

127

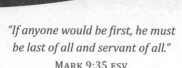
How to Be Great

*"If anyone would be first, he must
be last of all and servant of all."*
MARK 9:35 ESV

· ·

Jesus' disciples were a close-knit group. But like any family, they had disagreements. They struggled with pride, and this was one of those times. They'd just arrived in Capernaum. As they got settled in their temporary lodgings, Jesus noticed some tension. "What's up?" he asked. No one wanted to answer, but Jesus already knew. He'd heard the discussions while they traveled. They'd argued about—get this—which one of them was the greatest. Sounds like an echo from the back seats of a million car trips across the US.

Jesus sat down and scooped up a small child who was wandering around. Then he looked at His disciples and said, "If you want to be the best, you've got to be willing to be the least." Serving a newborn comes naturally to most of us. We want to care for their needs. But it's harder to serve teenagers, who roll their eyes and sass us. It's harder to serve other adults, who insult us and belittle our value. Still, it's in being a servant to all that we gain upward mobility on God's success ladder. It's in being humble that we become great.

*Serving others is hard, especially when I feel unappreciated. Help me
serve others with a joyful heart, and remind me to find my worth in You.*

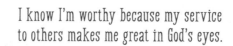

I know I'm worthy because my service
to others makes me great in God's eyes.

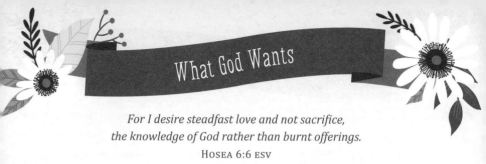

What God Wants

For I desire steadfast love and not sacrifice,
the knowledge of God rather than burnt offerings.
HOSEA 6:6 ESV

- -

The "mom" calendar can be overwhelming. Not only do we need to take care of our family's basic needs, but we commit to countless other things because they seem like good things. Ballet lessons and sports leagues and church classes. . . volunteering for community events. . .having coffee with friends to maintain important relationships. . .not to mention spending time at the gym.

There are many *good* things we can devote our time to. But let's not forget the *best* thing. God doesn't want us to be the perfect mom or the perfect wife or the perfect daughter or friend. More than anything, He just wants us to love Him. He wants us to make time in our calendars just to be with Him. And the more time we spend with Him, the easier it is to be and do all the things He wants us to be and do. The more we soak Him in, the more His love flows out of us, making us better moms and wives and friends.

Take a look at your calendar today. How much time are you spending in frantic service, trying to measure up to some invisible standard that can never be reached? Slow down. Spend time loving your Father, who already adores you, just as you are. More than anything, He wants your heart.

Show me how to slow down, be still, and soak in Your presence. I love You.

I know I'm worthy because God wants my heart.

Have Faith

And Jesus said to him, "What do you want me to do for you?"
And the blind man said to him, "Rabbi, let me recover my sight."
And Jesus said to him, "Go your way; your faith has made you well."
And immediately he recovered his sight and followed him on the way.

MARK 10:51–52 ESV

It's easy to convince ourselves that God wants us to do stuff for Him. He wants us to be good moms, wives, friends, and daughters. He wants us to be good employees and give 110 percent to our jobs. He wants us to be good citizens and volunteer for community events. Those are all worthy endeavors, but we must never count on those things to fulfill us or give us what we need. Time and again in God's Word, He commends faith. It's a simple trust that God will provide, that He will do for us what we can't do for ourselves. Ask yourself what you want and what you need. Have you talked to God about these things? When we believe and trust Him alone to work on our behalf, He will reward our faith. That doesn't mean He'll always give us what we ask for. But He will bless us beyond measure, in ways we can't imagine, when we trust Him.

Father, You know the unspoken needs of my heart. I trust
You alone to meet those needs. You are my only hope.

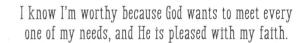
I know I'm worthy because God wants to meet every
one of my needs, and He is pleased with my faith.

130

Sow and Reap

Sow for yourselves righteousness; reap steadfast love;
break up our fallow ground, for it is the time to seek the LORD,
that h emay come and rain righteousness upon you.

HOSEA 10:12 ESV

• •

In this passage, God pleads with rebellious Israel to turn from her sin. Her poor choices led to disaster, and God wants her to come back to Him. He said, "When will you say, 'Enough is enough'? When will you realize your ways and habits aren't leading you to a good place? Turn around. Walk toward Me."

He uses language they would have understood—sowing and reaping is the language of an agricultural community. When a farmer sows, the harvest doesn't appear immediately. There's a lot of work and waiting that comes with the sowing process. They needed to do the hard task of breaking up the fallow ground of their hearts, which had become dry and hard. But when we seek God and His righteousness, He fills in the gaps. He sends His Holy Spirit to help with the heart process. And after a time, He will bring a harvest of love to those who seek Him.

What are you seeking today? What do you chase after? Seek Him alone. Run toward Him. In time, you'll reap the harvest you long for, and so much more.

I'm sorry for seeking fulfillment in the wrong places.
I want to turn around and run toward You. I know
You alone can provide the love and peace I desire.

I know I'm worthy because God already has a beautiful
harvest in store for me, and He's waiting to bless me.

Same God

When Daniel knew that the document had been signed, he went to his house where he had windows in his upper chamber open toward Jerusalem. He got down on his knees three times a day and prayed and gave thanks before his God, as he had done previously.

DANIEL 6:10 ESV

In this passage, some men are trying to get Daniel in trouble. They convinced the king to make a law that no one could worship anyone but the king. Anyone who broke this law would be thrown into a lions' den. Daniel responded to this crisis the way we should all respond to crises in our lives: he prayed.

He didn't try to hide his dependence on God. Instead, he knelt down right where he always did, in front of an open window. If you're familiar with the story, you know Daniel was, indeed, thrown into the lions' den, but he came out unscathed. God shut the lions' mouths and protected Daniel.

God is the same today as He was back then. He still sees us. He still cares about our hardships and trials. And He still protects us, rescues us, and shuts the lions' mouths. If there's one thing God notices, that gets His attention, it's faith. Daniel didn't let the crisis diminish his total belief that God is, and always will be, in control.

I know You are the same God who protected Daniel from the lions. Thank You for rescuing me from my own lions.

I know I'm worthy because God cares about each crisis I face, and He leads me through with confidence.

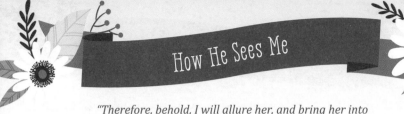

"Therefore, behold, I will allure her, and bring her into the wilderness, and speak tenderly to her. And there I will give her her vineyards and make the Valley of Achor a door of hope. And there she shall answer as in the days of her youth, as at the time when she came out of the land of Egypt."

HOSEA 2:14–15 ESV

• •

The book of Hosea tells the story of a young prophet who is called by God to marry a prostitute. Despite Hosea's love for her, she keeps returning to her sinful ways. This book of the Bible isn't a marriage manual. Rather, it paints a picture of God's patience and love toward us.

Like Hosea's wife, we mess up. Despite God's overwhelming love for us, we return to our old ways. Yet God's love for us is so deep, so all-consuming, He cannot give us up. He calls us back, wooing us into His arms.

Though God has every reason to be angry with us, He treats us gently, with mercy, because He loves us so much. If guilt and low self-esteem keep you stuck in a rut, remember, that's not what God sees when He looks at you. He sees a woman He adores, a woman He wants to take care of, a woman He wants to elevate to a high status. Let go of your past. Run into God's arms and become the woman He created you to be. That's already the way He sees you.

Thank You for seeing me for my potential, not for my past.

I know I'm worthy because God adores me.

Doing Surgery

"Come, let us return to the LORD; for he has torn us, that he may heal us; he has struck us down, and he will bind us up."

HOSEA 6:1 ESV

. . . .

The image of someone with a knife, waiting to cut us open, is the stuff of horror movies. But what if that person wears a surgical mask, and he's prepping to remove a cancerous growth? Yes, he will cut you open, but he's doing it to heal you.

God doesn't cause bad things to happen to us; He's too loving for that. But He does allow those hard circumstances in our lives. Hardship works like pruning shears, removing those things that keep us from becoming the people He intended us to be.

Motherhood can be hard. Life itself is full of twists and turns, many of them unpleasant. When you face difficulties, ask yourself, *How will God use this to remove the bad from my life? How will this help me grow into the person He meant me to be when He created me?*

Right now, you may feel like your soul is bleeding. But He will not leave you that way. He will bind you up, tend to your wounds, and stay with you while you heal. In the end, you will be strong. Courageous. Victorious. In the end, you'll look more like your Father, and that's a good thing. After all, you were created in His image.

I know You're doing a work in me, Father.
Please do it quickly. I will trust You as I heal.

> I know I'm worthy because God cares
> enough to remove bad things from my life.

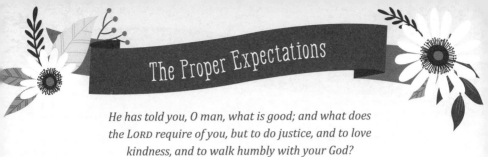

The Proper Expectations

He has told you, O man, what is good; and what does the LORD require of you, but to do justice, and to love kindness, and to walk humbly with your God?

MICAH 6:8 ESV

Being a mom these days comes with all the standard expectations: make sure your kids are clean, well fed, and loved. But social media brings the expectations to an entirely new level. You're supposed to look like a supermodel. Keep a beautiful, magazine-worthy home. Throw birthday parties on par with *Lifestyles of the Rich and Famous.*

When we look to the world for validation, we enter a never-ending merry-go-round where no one ever gets off and no one ever wins. God's requirements are fewer, simpler, and more straightforward.

Do justice. That means do the right thing, even when no one is looking.

Love kindness. Don't just fake it. Truly fall in love with being kind, so much so that you look for ways to show this to others and you get excited for the opportunities.

Walk humbly with your God. Remember who you are, who He is, and the miracle of having Him choose us. Talk to Him. Spend time with Him. Love Him completely.

Focus on those three things, and all the other expectations will somehow fall into their proper places.

Thank You for this reminder of Your clear expectations for me. Help me do justice, love kindness, and walk humbly with You.

I know I'm worthy because God helps me model the proper expectations for my children.

135

Generous

And he answered them, "Whoever has two tunics is to share with him who has none, and whoever has food is to do likewise."
LUKE 3:11 ESV

• •

If we're honest, most of us don't have everything we want. But also, if we're honest, most of us have more than we need. This verse addresses the more-than-you-need point of view, and it asks us to do something hard.

It's one thing to give out of your abundance. We clean out the clutter and get rid of the stained, the broken, or the out of date. We donate these things to charity and pat ourselves on the back. But that's not what God calls us to do. He wants us to be *generous.* Generosity refers to giving till it hurts a little.

If you have seven winter coats hanging in your closet—one for each outfit—you might consider sharing one or two of your favorites with someone who needs them. Instead of donating the out-of-date canned asparagus to the food pantry, donate a gift card so the director can stock up with what's most popular with clients.

Generosity doesn't come easily or naturally. If we want our children to grow up to be generous, we have to show them what that looks like. The blessings that come from giving to others far surpass any pleasure we receive from keeping it all for ourselves.

Teach me to be generous, Lord. Help me make generosity a habit in our home, so my children will embrace this character trait.

I know I'm worthy because my children learn from my actions.

The Struggle

And the devil took him up and showed him all the kingdoms of the world in a moment of time, and said to him, "To you I will give all this authority and their glory, for it has been delivered to me, and I give it to whom I will. If you, then, will worship me, it will all be yours."

LUKE 4:5–7 ESV

• •

It's easy to picture the devil as having a red suit, pointy ears, and a pitchfork. But the Bible tells us Satan disguises himself as an angel of light. He makes himself look beautiful and good and kind and benevolent, but he's a liar. If Jesus had worshipped him, Satan would not have delivered on his promise, or he would have taken it back, or the price would have been too high and Jesus would have been miserable.

Satan isn't creative. He still uses the same playbook. He still disguises himself as beautiful. He makes himself seem exciting. He says he can make all your dreams come true. And he's still a liar.

What things does Satan promise you? What does he tempt you with? Remember, he doesn't deliver on his promises. He might give a little bit, only to take it back. His intention is never for your good. His goal is to destroy you.

Say no. Run the other way. When your children see you struggling and winning over temptation, they learn that faith is worth the struggle.

Give me wisdom to recognize Satan. Give me strength to resist him.

I know I'm worthy because my struggles provide an example of godly living for my children to follow.

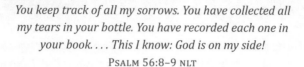

Tears in a Bottle

You keep track of all my sorrows. You have collected all my tears in your bottle. You have recorded each one in your book. . . . This I know: God is on my side!
PSALM 56:8–9 NLT

One of the loneliest things we can go through is crying alone. It's such a forlorn feeling when we don't think anyone knows or cares about our hurts. Yet God's Word tells us that's a feeling we never have to experience. God is our Father, and He cries when we cry. He not only wipes our tears, He stores them in a bottle. Our emotions are that precious to Him!

God cares about you deeply, individually. He knows everything that breaks your heart. He knows when you're frustrated and overwhelmed. He knows when you paste a smile on your face, though your heart is fractured. And He is so invested in you, He actually feels what you feel.

Next time you slip away to the bathroom stall to regain your composure, next time you cry into your pillow or weep when you're in the car by yourself, talk to God. Lean your head—and your heart—on His shoulder. He's right there soothing you, comforting you, and giving you courage to keep going when you don't think you can.

Thank You for caring about my feelings, God. Heal my hurts and let me feel Your presence. Give me strength to keep going.

I know I'm worthy because God collects my tears and gives me courage.

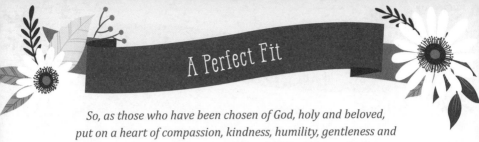

A Perfect Fit

So, as those who have been chosen of God, holy and beloved,
put on a heart of compassion, kindness, humility, gentleness and
patience; bearing with one another, and forgiving each other. . .
just as the Lord forgave you. . . . Beyond all these things put on love.
COLOSSIANS 3:12–14 NASB

God adopted us as daughters. It's like a fairy tale. . .we were hopeless without Him, but He came along and made us part of His royal family. Now, as royal daughters, He's given us a new wardrobe. He wants us to shed the old rags of bitterness, anger, fear, and pride. Those aren't suitable for a child of God. He wants us to wear only the best, most beautiful attitudes, so everyone can see who we are and *whose* we are!

It may take some practice as we get used to these new pieces in our character wardrobes. But as long as we seek God, spend time with Him each day, and do our best to please Him, He will send His Holy Spirit to work in our hearts. Over time, we'll find each item on this list to be a perfect fit, a perfect reflection of our new identity in Christ.

Lord, I want to look like You. I want the attitude I wear each day to be
a reflection of Your character, so others can see the family resemblance.
Help me develop these traits as I reflect Your love to those around me.

I know I'm worthy because God has chosen me to be like Christ!

Don't worry about the wicked or envy those who do wrong.
For like grass, they soon fade away. Like spring flowers,
they soon wither. Trust in the LORD and do good.
Then you will live safely in the land and prosper.
PSALM 37:1–3 NLT

It's hard not to play the comparison game. When you've sincerely tried to live for God and still struggle, it's tempting to look at others who haven't honored God, who seem to have it all. They have nicer cars. Nicer clothes. Their kids may seem better adjusted, their marriages stronger. But only God knows what goes on in a person's heart.

Remember, this life—the here and now—is only a blink compared to eternity. And God is watching. He will reward each of us for our actions. Those who live for this world will fade away, along with all their stuff. But those of us who choose to follow Him, even when it's hard, will be rewarded. God promises to bless us and prosper us, both now and for eternity. He also assures us that the wicked may prosper for a moment, but their success is short-lived.

Count the ways He's blessed you, and you'll run out of numbers. Stop comparing. God has good things in store for you.

Thank You for blessing me in more ways than I can count. I'm sorry
for comparing my life to others' lives. I know there's nothing better,
nothing more fulfilling, than a life lived to please You.

I know I'm worthy because God protects and prospers me!

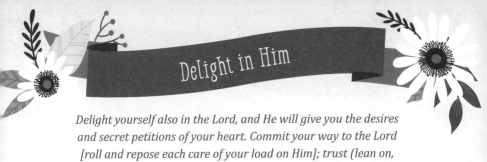

Delight in Him

Delight yourself also in the Lord, and He will give you the desires and secret petitions of your heart. Commit your way to the Lord [roll and repose each care of your load on Him]; trust (lean on, rely on, and be confident) also in Him and He will bring it to pass.
PSALM 37:4–5 AMPC

. . . .

Have you noticed that your children want to be like their friends? They want to dress like them, watch the same shows, and play the same games. It's natural to want to fit in with those you spend time with.

The same happens to us when we spend time with God. The more we hang out with Him through prayer, reading His Word, and praising Him, the more we'll want to be like Him. And as that happens, our desires will conform to His desires for us. When we delight in Him—when we're excited to spend time with Him, when we think He's the best thing that's ever happened to us, when we fall head-over-heels in love with Him—He will change our secret longings to match His. And then He'll give us those desires.

God wants to be our everything, and He wants to make our dreams come true. Delight in Him and see what happens.

Teach me to delight in You, Lord! I want my desires to match Your goals for me. Show me Your dreams for me and make those my longings as well. You are my everything.

I know I'm worthy because God grants me my secret heart's desire!

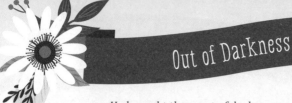

Out of Darkness

*He brought them out of darkness and the shadow of
death and broke apart the bonds that held them.*
PSALM 107:14 AMPC

• •

Have you ever driven in the dark and had your headlights go out? It's pretty scary. None of us wants to wander around in darkness, but it happens more often than you might think. We get bogged down in negative self-talk, and we believe the lies Satan whispers to us. We get trapped in fear and anxiety and depression, and our spirits get trapped in darkness. Some of us may feel chained to toxic, unhealthy habits or relationships, and we don't know how we'll ever find our way out.

But God is our hero. He hates to see His daughters and sons in bondage or trapped in darkness. Right now, He holds out His hand, waiting for you to take it. You may not know where He's leading, but you can be certain if you follow Him, you'll end up in a place of light and freedom. Cling to His hand. Praise Him in the darkness. With every breath, whisper a prayer. Hold on to Him with all your strength. You'll be glad you did.

*Lord, I feel like I've been wandering in darkness. My spirit
feels heavy and stifled. I know You're reaching for me right now,
and I'm reaching back for You. Thank You for leading me out of
this dark place, out of bondage, into Your freedom and light.*

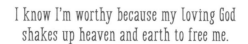

I know I'm worthy because my loving God
shakes up heaven and earth to free me.

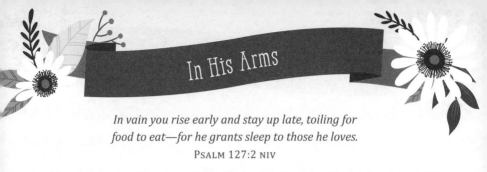

In His Arms

In vain you rise early and stay up late, toiling for
food to eat—for he grants sleep to those he loves.
PSALM 127:2 NIV

. . . .

Researchers say that men's brains are like egg cartons, while women's brains are like spaghetti—with everything all tangled and jumbled together. That's one reason men often sleep better than women. They can set everything aside and just sleep. Women often lie down, and when our bodies relax, our brains wake up. Sleep eludes us.

We can't be our best without good rest. It's important to protect our sleep. We can do practical things like avoiding caffeine after noon or exercising to tire our bodies out. But perhaps the most important thing we can do, when we finally rest our heads on our pillows, is turn our thoughts to God.

Talk to Him about your day. Tell Him about your troubles and concerns. Praise Him for your blessings. Rest in His presence and listen to His lullaby. He won't even be offended if You fall asleep in the middle of your prayer. He'll be delighted that you chose to end your day in His arms.

Lord, I'm exhausted. I need to sleep, but I just can't. So I'll spend this
time talking to You, listening to You, praising You. Let me feel Your
presence as You hold me in Your arms. You are my peace, and I love You.

I know I'm worthy because God takes care of me day and night.

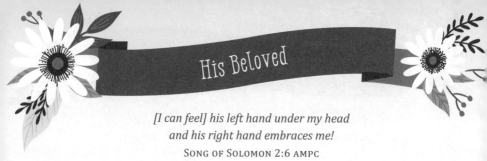

His Beloved

[I can feel] his left hand under my head
and his right hand embraces me!
SONG OF SOLOMON 2:6 AMPC

The Song of Solomon paints a picture of intimate, married love. Yet it's also a picture of how our Savior interacts with us. He adores us with passion. His love for us is personal and intimate.

God isn't just some big CEO who doesn't know his employees personally. He is in love with you. He cherishes you. He longs to spend time with you. He soaks in your thoughts, your dreams, your goals.

Close your eyes and try to feel His presence. Picture yourself in His embrace as He holds you sweetly, gently, intimately. Listen carefully. . . . What is He saying to you? What are the lyrics to His unique love song to you? With every breath, He's telling you that you are beautiful, you are valued, and you are loved.

With all the negative voices shouting from every direction, it's easy to miss the most important voice—the one who created you, who loves you, and who gave His life for you. In those moments when you feel forgotten, when you feel like nobody cares, take a moment to be still and feel His arms around you. You are His beloved.

Thank You for loving me with an all-consuming love.
When I feel lonely, rejected, or like nobody cares, remind
me of Your presence, and let me feel Your embrace.

I know I'm worthy because when I come to Him,
God embraces me in His all-encompassing love.

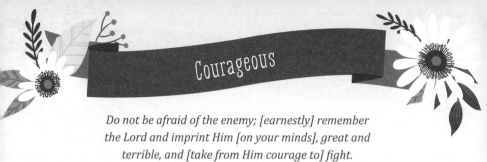

*Do not be afraid of the enemy; [earnestly] remember
the Lord and imprint Him [on your minds], great and
terrible, and [take from Him courage to] fight.*
NEHEMIAH 4:14 AMPC

. . . .

Nehemiah loved God and loved his people. He tried to lead the exiled Israelites back to Jerusalem to rebuild the wall and reclaim their rightful place. As you can imagine, neighboring countries weren't too crazy about that idea. They tried to stir things up by turning the Israelites against Nehemiah. They wrote letters. It was a full-on slander campaign.

Many would have said, "Forget it. It's not worth it." It would have been easy to just quit and find another job, but that's not what Nehemiah did. When the going got tough, he prayed. He gathered faithful men around him to guard the work they'd already done on the wall. He reminded people that God was on their side. And he told people to hang in there and find courage in the Lord.

When you know you're following God's will for your life and you meet opposition, pray. Surround yourself with faithful people. And speak God's Word every chance you get. Remind others and yourself that God is with you. Be strong. Take courage. And keep doing what God has called you to do.

*Lord, it's hard to be strong when it seems everyone is against
me. Surround me with people who will support my journey
with You. Give me strength to keep going, and help me
teach my children what faithful courage looks like.*

I know I'm worthy because God supplies all the courage I need.

Out of the Pit

I waited patiently for the Lord; and He inclined to me and heard my cry. He brought me up out of the pit of destruction, out of the miry clay, and He set my feet upon a rock making my footsteps firm.

PSALM 40:1–2 NASB

Being a mom is one of the most joyful, beautiful experiences in life. But it can also suck the life out of us if we're not careful. It's easy to pour ourselves into everyone else and forget to meet our own needs. Before long, we can end up emotionally drained, empty, unable to give to others.

When that happens, cry out to God. He will lean closer, wanting to hear the whispers of your heart. He loves you, and He will not leave you stranded in that pit. Close your eyes, take some deep breaths, and wait for His presence, His comfort, His peace. Talk to Him and tell Him what's on your mind. Gently, slowly, surely, He will lift you out of that murk and muck and set you on solid ground. Soon, you'll feel stronger, more confident. He'll guide you for the next steps, giving you wisdom and courage to keep going.

Call on Him and wait patiently. He is already on His way to rescue you.

I know You love me, Lord. I know You're ready to fill me up even before I'm empty. Thank You for being my rescuer, my courage, and my peace.

I know I'm worthy because my God pulls me up,
sets me on solid ground, and steadies my steps.

Keep Asking

"Keep on asking, and you will receive what you ask for. Keep on seeking, and you will find. Keep on knocking, and the door will be opened to you. For everyone who asks, receives. Everyone who seeks, finds. And to everyone who knocks, the door will be opened."

MATTHEW 7:7–8 NLT

Anyone who's been a parent for less than twenty-four hours knows the frustration of being awakened by hungry cries. Even an infant knows to keep calling out until dinner arrives—or a clean diaper or soothing arms and a lullaby. God's Word tells us in Matthew 18 to be like a little child, and here we're told to be persistent in telling God our needs.

Your Father loves you. He *longs* for your presence. He *wants* you to spend time with Him. Sometimes He grants a request right away. But most of the time, He wants us to keep asking, keep praying, keep trusting. . . . In so doing, we naturally draw closer to Him.

We can ask with confidence, knowing that He wants good things for us even more than we want them for ourselves. When we ask for things that He wants too, He will certainly answer our prayers. Keep praying. Your Father adores you, and He wants to bless you.

Sweet Father, thank You for hearing my prayers. Thank You for listening to every word I say. Help me line up my desires with what You want for my life. Give me patience to wait for Your best for me. I love You.

I know I'm worthy because my loving God opens the door to my desires.

147

Wait on the Lord

Many crave and seek the ruler's favor, but the
wise man [waits] for justice from the Lord.
PROVERBS 29:26 AMPC

Time and again in God's Word, we're told to wait. Perhaps the reason we're given that command so often is because we need to hear it again and again. Waiting isn't easy for anyone. It's not easy for our children, and it's not easy for us.

When things don't go the way we want them to, it's easy to try and step in front of God. We don't think He's working fast enough, or we don't like what He's doing. So instead of waiting, we call people with power over the situation or manipulate things to go our way. The problem is, we don't see the big picture like God does. Our "solutions" often breed bigger problems.

God loves us, and He is always working on our behalf. He is eternal, and He has had eternity to address your specific situation. What He wants now is your trust. Instead of trying to fix things on your own, seek God. Trust Him. He won't let you down.

Father, I'm sorry for moving in front of You and trying to work things out
for myself. I know you want me to stay calm and wait on You. When I'm
anxious and frustrated, give me patience and peace as I trust Your timing.

I know I'm worthy because I'm a wise woman
who knows God will make all things right.

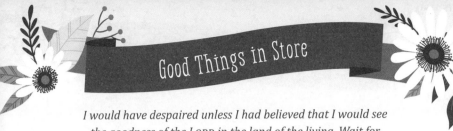

Good Things in Store

*I would have despaired unless I had believed that I would see
the goodness of the LORD in the land of the living. Wait for
the LORD; be strong and let your heart take courage.*
PSALM 27:13–14 NASB

• •

When we look at our children and how quickly they grow and change, life seems like a fast-paced roller coaster. But in troubled times, each day can seem eternal. We may wonder if life will ever be good again.

David must have felt that way when he hid in caves with Saul in hot pursuit. David was tired and hungry. He'd done nothing wrong, yet the king wanted him dead. It was during this time David wrote these words: "Be strong and let your heart take courage." In the middle of the worst trials he'd faced, he believed God had good things in store for this life. Eventually, David became king.

When we're struggling, it's easy to forget our Father loves us. He has wonderful things in store for us, not just for eternity, but in this life as well. Many times, God refers to Himself as the God of hope. Hope is the promise, the belief, that good things are coming.

When you're overwhelmed, when despair cloaks your spirit like a heavy blanket, take courage. Wait on the Lord, the God of hope. Good things are coming your way.

*I'm overwhelmed. Give me courage, Lord. Show Your me
goodness soon. I need Your presence and Your love.*

I know I'm worthy because God has something good waiting for me.

Learning to Trust Him

*Our inner selves wait [earnestly] for the Lord; He is our Help
and our Shield. For in Him does our heart rejoice, because
we have trusted (relied on and been confident) in His holy
name. Let Your mercy and loving-kindness, O Lord, be upon
us, in proportion to our waiting and hoping for You.*
PSALM 33:20–22 AMPC

• •

Experience is one thing that cannot be rushed. It takes time, patience, and wading through the rough waters of life. The good thing is, the more stuff we go through, the easier it is to understand God's faithfulness. We can look back on trial after trial and see how He's held our heads above water, how He's led us not only through but out of the tempest. We can see how He's allowed us to find success and joy and happiness after the storm.

When you face hard things, wait for God. Expect great things. Watch to see how He will bring you through with victory. Learning to trust God takes experience, and that's what you're getting each time you go through something difficult. Trust Him. He will take care of you. He has good things waiting on the other side.

*Father, when I face difficult times, my anxiety kicks into high gear.
But each time, You show Your faithfulness. Each time, my faith grows
stronger. Teach me to wait for You, trust You, and rest in You.*

I know I'm worthy because Almighty God helps and shields me.

150

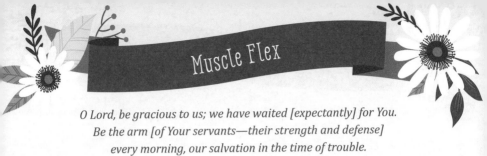

Muscle Flex

O Lord, be gracious to us; we have waited [expectantly] for You.
Be the arm [of Your servants—their strength and defense]
every morning, our salvation in the time of trouble.
ISAIAH 33:2 AMPC

Have you ever faced a bully? Schoolyard tyrants are common in elementary and junior high schools. Even adults face people and problems that seem overpowering. But let's say, while that bully is taunting you, Arnold Schwarzenegger shows up. He doesn't say a word, just eyes the bully and flexes those giant muscles of his. Chances are pretty good that bully will back off, slinking into the shadows.

As daughters of the King, we have a stronger arm than the *Terminator* star. We don't have to wonder if or when He will show up; He promised to never leave us. When you face the giants, wait expectantly for God's shadow as He stands behind you, flexes His muscles, and stares down your enemies. He is your Father, and He doesn't like it when the enemy messes with His children.

Take heart. No one can stand against the Almighty God.

Thank You, Father, for being my strength and my defense.
Right now, I feel overwhelmed, and I face giants I can't overcome
on my own. I'm so grateful I don't have to stand alone. Even if I
don't see You or feel You, I'll remain strong, knowing You are right
behind me, flexing Your muscle, and working on my behalf.

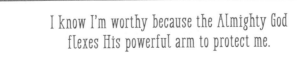

I know I'm worthy because the Almighty God
flexes His powerful arm to protect me.

Valuable

"What is the price of five sparrows—two copper coins?
Yet God does not forget a single one of them. And the very
hairs on your head are all numbered. So don't be afraid;
you are more valuable to God than a whole flock of sparrows."

LUKE 12:6–7 NLT

. . . .

It doesn't matter how many children you have. To your mom heart, each one is unique and treasured. One may have freckles, another may be boisterous, another may be a shy bookworm. But to you, Mom, each one takes your breath away.

That's how God feels about you! You are His. He created you. Before time began, He thought you up. He decided the color of your eyes and how tall you'd be. He sketched out your strengths. He even threw in a healthy dash of hopes and dreams unique to you. He adores you, just as you are. He laughs when you laugh and cries when you cry.

Knowing what you mean to your Father, why would you be anxious about anything? He cares for you tenderly, intimately, and individually. Relax. Trust Him. When it comes to your life, He has everything under control.

Father, I often forget my value in Your eyes. But when I think of how
much I love my children, I'm reminded that You love me even more.
Thank You for caring about even the small things in my life. I'm sorry
for doubting You. Today, I choose to trust You and relax in Your love.

I know I'm worthy because God values me above all else!

His Goodness

Upon him was the good hand of his God. For Ezra had prepared and set his heart to seek the Law of the Lord [to inquire for it and of it, to require and yearn for it], and to do. . . . I was strengthened and encouraged, for the hand of the Lord my God was upon me.
EZRA 7:9–10, 28 AMPC

· ·

We all want God's good hand on us and on our children. But sometimes His blessings seem to elude us. Christ said in John 16:33 (NIV) that "in this world you will have trouble." Though hard times are a normal part of life, Ezra gives us a formula to experience more of God's goodness. We're to seek God, spend time reading His Word, and do what it says.

When we set our hearts on God. . .when we allow ourselves to crave Him, and we spend every moment with Him at the center of our thoughts. . .when we long for His Word so much that we think about it all day. . .when we sincerely do our best to obey Him. . .wow! That opens up the floodgates! God is pleased with a heart that sincerely seeks Him. When we do this, He gives us strength. He gives us courage. And He pours out His goodness on us.

Father, I long for You. With all my heart, I want to be with You. I want to feel Your presence each moment. Walk with me. Take my hand and lead me. Thank You for Your goodness in my life.

I know I'm worthy because God has put His good hand upon me.

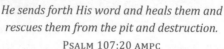

The Most We Can Do

*He sends forth His word and heals them and
rescues them from the pit and destruction.*
PSALM 107:20 AMPC

· ·

When we hear of others' hardships, we want to help. Yet we may struggle to know what to do for them. Apart from baking a casserole, there's often not a lot we can do. That's when we say, "At least I can pray." Yet those are perhaps the most flawed words we can utter.

Prayer is always the *most* we can do. It's never the *least* we can do. God's Word has power. When we don't know what to pray, we can pray scriptures, reminding Him of His promises. When we pray, believing God hears and will act, that belief impresses God. Our faith moves Him to act. Though He doesn't always answer our prayers the way we want Him to, He often does. Sometimes His solution is even better than we imagined.

When you or someone you know faces trials, pray. Let your children see you pray. Invite them to join you! And remind them, again and again, that prayer is never the least. It's always the most important way we can bring about change.

*Lord, thank You for hearing my prayers. Thank You for answering.
You are my only hope. You know the needs in my heart, Father.
Speak the Word. Heal the sick, comfort the hurting, and open doors
that need to be opened. I trust You, and I know You will answer.*

I know I'm worthy because God's Word
and my prayers surpass all powers.

Living in Love

*We know (understand, recognize, are conscious of,
by observation and by experience) and believe (adhere to and
put faith in and rely on) the love God cherishes for us. God
is love, and he who dwells and continues in love dwells and
continues in God, and God dwells and continues in him.*

1 JOHN 4:16 AMPC

Think of your best friend. Maybe it's your spouse, your sister, or a lifelong friend. A best friend is someone you want to hang out with, someone who will stick with you for the long haul.

God wants to be your best friend. He adores you. This verse says you are cherished. And right here, in this verse, He gives His address. He wants you to come and hang out with Him in His dwelling place.

When we treat others with love, we meet Him in His dwelling place. When we consistently act with love by showing patience, kindness, goodness, and self-control, we continue in Him—and that makes Him want to continue hanging around us.

God is love. Love is who He is and where He lives. More than anything, He wants us to live there with Him.

*I know You love me, Father. I also know You want me to love
others in a way that invites them into Your presence. Help me
live in Your love. I want to spend every moment with You.*

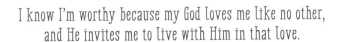

I know I'm worthy because my God loves me like no other,
and He invites me to live with Him in that love.

God's Word

*The entrance and unfolding of Your words give light; their
unfolding gives understanding (discernment and comprehension)
to the simple. . . . Establish my steps and direct them by [means
of] Your word; let not any iniquity have dominion over me.*
PSALM 119:130, 133 AMPC

• •

God's Word has always been available to His people. But before the invention
of the printing press, most believers didn't have their own copies. In fact, many
couldn't read, so in order to know God's Word, they had to have it read to them
at a temple or worship service.

Now look at us! Not only does modern printing make God's Word accessible
to the masses, but the internet allows us to carry the entire Bible, in multiple
translations, right on our phones. We can even have it read to us out loud.

God's Word holds power and light. It changes lives. Yet many of us rarely read
it. If you were given a few million dollars to spend how you wanted, wouldn't you
take advantage of the gift? The Bible is a far greater treasure than any amount of
money. Make it a point to spend time reading, learning, and absorbing His Word,
every single day.

*Thank You for Your Word, Father. I know it's not just some
dusty words. It's a living, active, powerful thing. Help me read
Your Word every day. I want to absorb it into my thoughts,
my mind, my skin. I want Your Word to direct my path.*

I know I'm worthy because God has blessed me with His Word.

Miracle Worker

The LORD said to Abraham, "Why did Sarah laugh?
Why did she say, 'Can an old woman like me have a baby?'
Is anything too hard for the LORD? I will return about
this time next year, and Sarah will have a son."
GENESIS 18:13–14 NLT

• •

God promised Abraham's descendants would be more numerous than the stars. Yet he and Sarah were approaching one hundred, and they had yet to conceive a child. Sarah probably thought she misunderstood the promise. Surely, at age ninety, her time for childbearing had passed. But nothing is too hard for God. It wasn't too hard back then, and it's not too hard today.

What impossible thing do you face? What difficult trial seems taller than any mountain? What hardship seems to wash over you like a flood, stealing your breath, drowning your hope? Don't be like Sarah and laugh at God's promises. Claim them! Believe them! Take them seriously.

Nothing is too hard for God. He's in the miracle business. His next miracle may just be in you.

Father, You know what I'm feeling. You know what I face.
Right now, it's easier to scoff than to hope, because what if You don't
follow through? Yet I know, more than I know anything, that You love me.
You want to work miracles in my life. Thank You for answering Sarah's
prayers for a child, and thank You for answering my prayers as well.

I know I'm worthy because God does the
impossible—in, with, and through me.

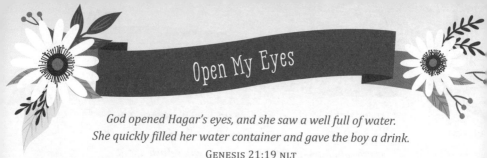

Open My Eyes

God opened Hagar's eyes, and she saw a well full of water.
She quickly filled her water container and gave the boy a drink.
GENESIS 21:19 NLT

When God promised Sarah and Abraham a child, Sarah thought they were too old. She told Abraham to sleep with her much-younger servant, Hagar. Hagar gave birth to Ishmael, but Sarah got jealous. Later, when Isaac was born, Sarah sent Hagar and Ishmael away, into the desert. Hagar had no choice in any of this, and yet she was left destitute, with no way to care for her young son.

No matter your circumstances, no matter what's brought you to this point, God loves you. He hears your cries, and He will take care of your needs. He may meet these needs in unexpected ways. Open your eyes! Look around, expecting God to work. Remember, hope is the opposite of fear. Hope is the belief that good things are coming, while fear is the expectation of bad things. Cling to God and the knowledge that He adores you, He understands your concerns, and He will take care of you.

Thank You, Father, for seeing me and caring about what I'm going
through. I know You will take care of my needs. Open my eyes to
Your unique, unexpected solutions to my problems. I love You,
I trust You, and I know You are good. All my hope is in You.

I know I'm worthy because God opens my
eyes to what He has prepared for me.

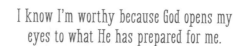

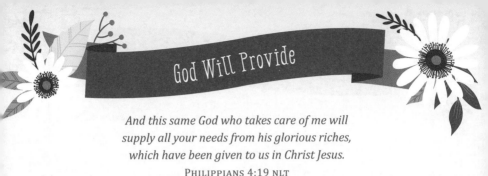

God Will Provide

*And this same God who takes care of me will
supply all your needs from his glorious riches,
which have been given to us in Christ Jesus.*
PHILIPPIANS 4:19 NLT

One of the names of God in the Bible is Yahweh-Yireh, which means *the Lord will provide.* God loves you, and He wants to be your provider. In Latin, the word "provide" indicates a certain foresight. It's not an after-the-fact, caught-off-guard scramble to make do. It's a calculated preparation, looking ahead at future needs and making sure everything is in place to meet those needs beforehand.

Remember, God has already seen the future. He exists in eternity, which means He's already been to the future! That's hard for us to understand with our limited view of time, but God doesn't have the same limitations. He knew about your need long before you did, and He has already made provision for it. This verse holds a promise, not a wish. He *will* supply all your needs. His riches are unending, and He is generous with His children.

Do you have a need and are unsure how it will be met? Don't be anxious. Instead, get excited. Wait like a kid at Christmas, knowing God will surprise you with something wonderful, something perfect for the occasion. He will meet your needs in ways you could never anticipate.

*Thank You for supplying all my needs, Father.
I trust You fully. I can't wait to see how You'll provide.*

I know I'm worthy because God supplies all my needs.

God of Comfort

God. . .comforts and encourages and refreshes
and cheers the depressed and the sinking.
2 Corinthians 7:6 ampc

. . . .

We humans are creatures of comfort. When the going gets tough, we often find the closest thing to make us feel better, right away. It may be a tub of chocolate ice cream or a supersized order of fries. We may binge-watch a favorite television show or pay for a massage or a manicure. Many turn to excessive shopping, alcohol, or drugs for comfort. Though all these may provide temporary relief, the feeling doesn't last.

When you feel blue, go to God, the only lasting source of hope. When it seems you'll drown in the deep waters of depression or anxiety, dive into His Word. He is there to listen, to encourage, and to lift you out of that dark place. He will set you on a high rock, wipe your tears, and wrap you in His love and assurance. At just the right moment, He will send a gentle breeze, a friend's phone call, or a stranger's encouraging smile. He'll remind you that He sees you and you're important to Him. He'll lift your chin and give you a reason to smile.

I'm struggling, Lord. I know I have so much to be grateful for:
my children, my family, my friends. But I need Your
comfort right now. Thank You for seeing me.

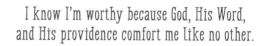

I know I'm worthy because God, His Word,
and His providence comfort me like no other.

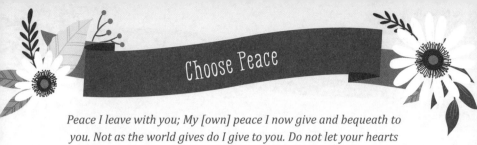

Choose Peace

Peace I leave with you; My [own] peace I now give and bequeath to you. Not as the world gives do I give to you. Do not let your hearts be troubled, neither let them be afraid. [Stop allowing yourselves to be agitated and disturbed; and do not permit yourselves to be fearful and intimidated and cowardly and unsettled.]

JOHN 14:27 AMPC

• •

When you think of peace, what picture comes to mind? Perhaps you're sitting in a chair on the beach, immersed in a good book, iced tea close at hand, waves crashing in the distance. Or maybe you're cuddled in a soft blanket in front of a roaring fire, watching snow fall outside your window. These settings may provide temporary peace, but they do little to silence those disturbing thoughts that upset your frame of mind. Only God can do that.

But living in His peace takes discipline. He says we're not to *let* our hearts be troubled. That indicates that we have some control over those troubling thoughts. While we can't dictate which thoughts enter our minds, we can certainly choose which ones we sit in. When stressful things invade your brain, push them back. Tell them *no.* Shift your thoughts to Christ, His goodness, and His love. Sink into His Words, claim His promises, and dwell in His peace.

I need to feel Your peace right now, Father. Teach me to select Your peace instead of my anxiety. Your peace lives in me, and I choose to live in it.

I know I'm worthy because Jesus gives me peace beyond understanding.

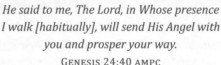

Finding Success

He said to me, The Lord, in Whose presence
I walk [habitually], will send His Angel with
you and prosper your way.
GENESIS 24:40 AMPC

· ·

In this story, Abraham sent his servant back to his hometown to find a wife for his son Isaac. He didn't want Isaac marrying a girl from Canaan, where they currently lived, because the Canaanites didn't worship God. He told his servant, "God will send an angel before you. He'll make sure you find success."

When the servant arrived, he prayed and asked God to show him the right girl. Sure enough, God made it clear, and Rebekah went with him willingly.

Sometimes we act like success depends only on us. We do play a part in our success: just as the servant had to be obedient and make that long journey, we must do the work that's required. But when we've done all we can do, it's time to pray. Each step along the way, it's time to pray. When we seek God, talk to Him often, and trust His guidance, He will open doors we thought couldn't be opened. He will prosper us and help us succeed.

I want to be successful, Lord, as a mother, daughter, wife, friend,
employee. . . . But the most important way I can succeed is by
pleasing You. Remind me to walk with You and talk with You about
everything. You are my only hope, and I will follow where You lead.

I know I'm worthy because as I walk with God, He grants me success.

The Life Source

Dwell in Me, and I will dwell in you. [Live in Me, and I will live in you.]. . . I am the Vine; you are the branches. Whoever lives in Me and I in him bears much (abundant) fruit. However, apart from Me [cut off from vital union with Me] you can do nothing.
JOHN 15:4–5 AMPC

Have you ever trimmed a bush? Perhaps you cut back a wandering rosebush or trimmed the hedges around your house. What happens to the trimmed bits after they're removed from the bush? That's right. They die, because they're no longer connected to the life source.

Christ is our life source. When we remain in Him through daily conversation and reading His Word, our spirits thrive. Things may not be perfect, but in Him, we are strong. We bear fruit in others' lives. But when we go a day or two without spending time with Him, we start to shrivel from dehydration. And if we permanently disconnect, our spirits will die. We're as spiritually useless as those dead branches.

Christ loves us, and He wants us to thrive! Stay in Him. Pray continually as you go through your day. Spend time in His Word, learning what He has to say. Do these things, and He'll supply you with love, peace, joy, and everything else you need for a full, abundant life.

I want to live in You and bear much fruit. Live in me, Jesus.

I know I'm worthy because I live in God and He lives in me.

163

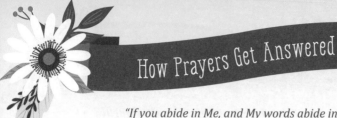

How Prayers Get Answered

"If you abide in Me, and My words abide in you,
ask whatever you wish, and it will be done for you."
JOHN 15:7 NASB

Do you ever give specific instructions to your children? *First, do your homework. Then, clean your room. If you do these things before dinner, we'll go out for ice cream later!* In this passage, Christ makes it as easy as possible to understand how to have our prayers answered the way we want.

First, we must abide in Him. That means we talk to Him all the time about everything that happens to us. We consult Him for decisions. We tell Him our joys and sorrows. He longs to have a close relationship with us, and talking to Him sets that up.

Second, we must listen to Him. We do this by reading His Word, learning what He says, and thinking about how His thoughts impact our lives. When we do both of these things consistently—abide in Him and let His Words abide in us—a transformation happens. Our desires become united with His desires. That's when our prayers produce crazy-wonderful, miracle-status results.

This isn't a formula for a never-ending wish list. Instead, it's a promise: if we live in Him and He lives in us, His power will show up in response to our prayers.

I want to live each moment in You, Lord. I want Your Words to live in me.

I know I'm worthy because as I dwell in Jesus and His words in me,
God changes my desires to match His, and He grants my requests.

The Dwelling Place

"My Father's house has many rooms; if that were not so,
would I have told you that I am going there to prepare a place
for you? And if I go and prepare a place for you, I will come back
and take you to be with me that you also may be where I am."
JOHN 14:2–3 NIV

Do you dream of having a big fancy house? Large homes are nice, but they take longer to clean. Since the house Jesus prepares for us won't collect the clutter we have here on earth, hopefully the housekeeping responsibilities will be minimal. One thing we can know for sure—if He is building it, it will be amazing!

While we wait for move-in day, we can still live with Him daily. The Holy Spirit is right here, living with us, walking with us, traveling each step of the journey with us. And one day, Christ will come back and take us to the place He's prepared. That's not a pie-in-the-sky fantasy. It's a promise. And God always keeps His promises.

Today, as you take care of your own household duties, remember you already live in a royal palace, because you are the daughter of the King. And one day, you'll dwell with Him in person forever.

Thank You for preparing a place for me with You,
Father. And thank You for living with me now.

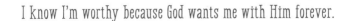

I know I'm worthy because God wants me with Him forever.

Walk This Way

He will surely be gracious to you at the sound of your cry;
when He hears it, He will answer you. . . . And your ears will
hear a word behind you, saying, This is the way; walk in it,
when you turn to the right hand and when you turn to the left.
ISAIAH 30:19, 21 AMPC

Have you ever felt overwhelmed, not knowing what to do next? Most of us feel that way on a daily basis, especially when it comes to parenting. It would be nice if life came with a detailed instruction manual addressing each possible scenario with directions for how to navigate.

The Bible may not specifically talk about all situations, but its wisdom applies to anything we face. And wherever we are, whatever we encounter, the Holy Spirit is always close by. He hears our inner cries. When we seek Him, when we ask Him for direction, He gives it.

Listen for that inner whisper—that still, small voice that says, "Do this," or "Don't do that." Be faithful and obedient to that voice, knowing He will never steer you in the wrong direction.

I need Your help, Lord. I'm overwhelmed, and I feel frozen. I have no
idea how to respond to my current situation. Take my hand and show
me which way to go. Thank You for hearing my cries and answering.

I know I'm worthy because God directs my steps as I walk closer to Him.

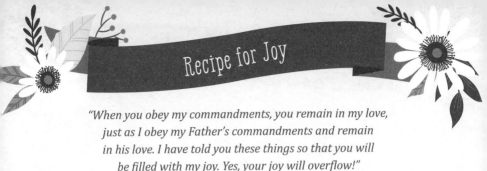

Recipe for Joy

"When you obey my commandments, you remain in my love, just as I obey my Father's commandments and remain in his love. I have told you these things so that you will be filled with my joy. Yes, your joy will overflow!"
JOHN 15:10–11 NLT

Do you know the difference between happiness and joy? Many people confuse the two, and it's easy to do. But there's a simple way to tell the difference: Happiness is based on current circumstances. Joy is based on the future.

That's why we can feel happy one moment, and in an instant that happiness can dissipate. We may feel blissfully happy sitting in a movie theater with our family, waiting to enjoy the show. But if the person behind you spills a drink down your back, your happiness will turn to frustration right away!

Joy, on the other hand, is more permanent. It's based on our relationship with God and our knowledge that He will never leave us or forsake us. It's based on our assurance that He's preparing a place for us and we'll spend eternity with Him. No temporary circumstance can take that away.

Obey Him. Live in His presence. Love Him with all your heart, and love others like you're looking out for your own personal needs by doing so. This kind of commitment will create a permanent, underlying joy, no matter the circumstance.

Teach me to obey You and remain in Your love, Father.

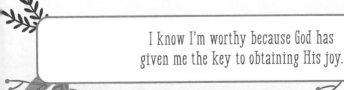

I know I'm worthy because God has
given me the key to obtaining His joy.

Using Your Skills

And let the beauty and delightfulness and favor of the Lord our
God be upon us; confirm and establish the work of our hands—
yes, the work of our hands, confirm and establish it.
PSALM 90:17 AMPC

What kinds of things do you do better than others? In what areas do you thrive? God created each of us with unique gifts and talents to share. Some of us are super organized. Others are creative. Some love to cook, while others love to write. Whatever you're good at, don't keep those skills to yourself. God blesses us with different abilities so we can bless others and glorify God.

There's no point in comparing our abilities to others. If we were all musicians, who would preach and teach? If we were all athletes, who would write books? This world needs builders, childcare workers, and cooks. It needs encouragers and compassion givers and people who will call it like they see it. And each of those gifts, talents, and skills should be wrapped in love as we share them with others.

Ask God to "confirm and establish" the works of your hands today, as you use your abilities to love others and love God.

Father, it's easy to compare my abilities to others' gifts
and talents. Show me what I do well and guide me to
use what You've given me in a way that honors You.

I know I'm worthy because God has called me and
equipped me with skills to use for Him in this world.

Invincible

The Lord God is my Strength, my personal bravery, and my invincible army; He makes my feet like hinds' feet and will make me to walk [not to stand still in terror, but to walk] and make [spiritual] progress upon my high places [of trouble, suffering, or responsibility]!

HABAKKUK 3:19 AMPC

• •

Think about the time you felt the strongest, the bravest, and the most invincible. Maybe it was just after you'd given birth. Or perhaps it was when you'd reached a specific goal or overcome some obstacle. That is who you are. That is who God created you to be.

God didn't give us a spirit of fear or anxiety (see 2 Timothy 1:7). He created us in His image, and He is strong, brave, and invincible. On our own, we might not be very impressive. But with Him living inside us, we take on His qualities.

What in your life makes you fearful or anxious? Stop looking at it from your point of view and try to see it from God's perspective. That giant isn't too big to defeat—he's too big to miss. That mountain isn't too heavy to move—one flick of His finger will crumble it to the ground. That person or situation cannot stand against God Almighty, and God Almighty lives in you!

Take my fear, Lord, and replace it with Your strength. Guide my steps. Make me brave. I know nothing is impossible for You.

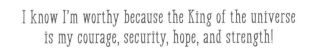

I know I'm worthy because the King of the universe is my courage, security, hope, and strength!

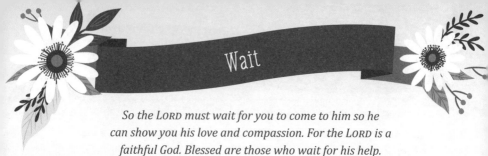

Wait

*So the LORD must wait for you to come to him so he
can show you his love and compassion. For the LORD is a
faithful God. Blessed are those who wait for his help.*
ISAIAH 30:18 NLT

. . . .

Most moms have lived through a frustrated toddler moment, when their child wants what they want, and they want it right now. If we're honest, most of us have those moments pretty often— we've just learned to control our tantrums a little better. But patience is important to God. It's one of the fruits of the Spirit. God is a patient God, and one of His main goals is for us to become like Him.

When a toddler throws a fit, we often wait for them to calm down before we move forward with our plans. God is a loving parent, and He wants to bless us. But He will wait for us to be still, to be calm, to be patient. He wants us to trust Him, even when we must wait.

What are you asking God for right now? Waiting is hard, but those who wait, knowing God will deliver something amazing, are blessed. Remember, God loves you. He is faithful, and He keeps all His promises. Take some deep breaths, tell God how grateful you are for the work He's doing on your behalf, and wait. Good things are on the way.

*Thank You for Your faithfulness. I know You
have good things in store. Teach me to wait.*

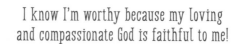

I know I'm worthy because my loving
and compassionate God is faithful to me!

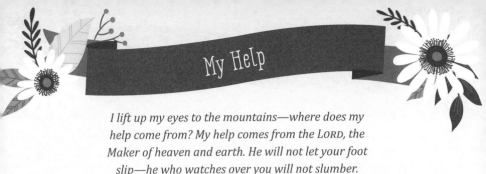

My Help

I lift up my eyes to the mountains—where does my help come from? My help comes from the LORD, the Maker of heaven and earth. He will not let your foot slip—he who watches over you will not slumber.
PSALM 121:1–3 NIV

• •

Some of the earliest lessons we teach our children are the value of hard work and the value of being prepared. These values serve us well in adulthood as they help us find and keep a good job, pay our bills, and prepare for what's ahead.

While these are good lessons, we must never rely on those things to take care of us. Hard workers still lose their jobs sometimes. Those who have planned for the worst may still find themselves in a horrible situation—one they *didn't* plan for.

We must never forget that God alone is our help. No high-salary job or fancy retirement plan comes close to His care for us. We should work hard but stay humble enough to understand who we are and who God is. When we have those priorities in the right order, our jobs become a way to serve Him and others, not our salvation. Everything we have—our homes, our cars, our IRAs—become simply tools to use in kingdom work.

He is the source of everything we need, and He will never let us down.

Thank You for being my help and my salvation for all things. Thank You for watching out for me, for staying close by, and for rescuing me when I need it.

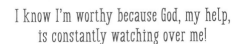

I know I'm worthy because God, my help, is constantly watching over me!

171

Who He Is

I have made Your Name known to them and revealed Your character and Your very Self, and I will continue to make [You] known, that the love which You have bestowed upon Me may be in them [felt in their hearts] and that I [Myself] may be in them.
JOHN 17:26 AMPC

• •

Has your child ever asked you a question you couldn't answer? Perhaps you knew the answer, but you didn't know how to explain it in an age-appropriate way. But there's a good chance your child asked something you didn't know, so you explained it as best you could, knowing your explanation was limited.

We can't ever really know everything about God. We may have an idea about who He is and what He's like, but our minds aren't big enough to fully comprehend God's character. Jesus knew this, so He tried to make it as simple as possible for us. He said, "If you want to know God, look at me" (see John 14:9).

Look at how Jesus interacted with others. When others judged, He showed compassion. When others ignored, He paid attention. When others were self-important, He was humble. He stood for what is right and refused to let others be taken advantage of. He freed the entrapped, healed the sick, and befriended the lonely. Everything Christ did reflected who God is: He is love.

Show me who You are, Lord, and make me like You.

I know I'm worthy because God has revealed
Himself to me and poured His love into my heart.

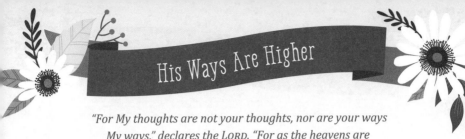

His Ways Are Higher

*"For My thoughts are not your thoughts, nor are your ways
My ways," declares the LORD. "For as the heavens are
higher than the earth, so are My ways higher than your
ways and My thoughts than your thoughts."*
ISAIAH 55:8–9 NASB

. . . .

When your toddler wants to play on a busy street and you don't let him, he may throw a fit. In his mind, you're preventing him from having fun. He may be angry with you, but you stand your ground, because your thoughts are higher than your toddler's thoughts. He doesn't understand the danger, but you do.

Compared to God, our minds are kind of like a toddler's. God knows things we can't possibly understand. He adores us, and all His actions are driven by love. Part of becoming a mature Christian is the ability to calmly place our faith in Him even when things don't make sense to us. No matter what, we can trust Him, knowing that He is love and all His ways are good.

The more we talk to Him and spend time in His Word, the more access He gives us to His thoughts, and trust becomes easier. Spend time with Him each day. Ask Him to show you who He is and how He thinks. And when you don't understand, be still, rest in His love, and trust His heart.

*I want to know You, Lord. Show me Your ways. Teach me Your
thoughts. And when I don't understand, help me trust You anyway.*

I know I'm worthy because through His Word,
God gives me access to His higher mind.

Day and Night

GOD went ahead of them in a Pillar of Cloud during the day to guide them on the way, and at night in a Pillar of Fire to give them light. . . . The Pillar of Cloud by day and the Pillar of Fire by night never left the people.
EXODUS 13:21–22 MSG

• •

We often hear stories about how God guided someone through their darkest hour. These are remarkable stories of faith and trust, but we don't have to wait for things to get dark and scary to look to God. He is there to lead us through the dark and the light, the dusk and the dawn. He gives us wisdom about the big stuff and the small stuff. No matter what we face, He is there, holding out His hand, providing His light and leading the way.

It's easy to forget about Him when there's plenty of light, when things are easy and we're not facing hardship or trials. But many trials can be avoided by staying close to Him. No matter the circumstance, look to Him. Seek His guidance, knowing He will never steer you wrong.

I'm guilty of waiting for the darkest hour to call out to You, Lord. But that's not the way I want to live. Take my hand now, and don't let me go. I want to cling to You in good times and bad, when the path is smooth and when it's rocky. Thank You for staying near me, for leading me, and for never letting me go.

I know I'm worthy because God guides me day and night.

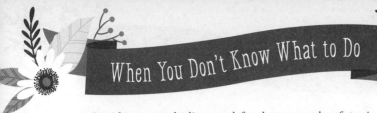

When You Don't Know What to Do

David was greatly distressed, for the men spoke of stoning
him because the souls of them all were bitterly grieved,
each man for his sons and daughters. But David encouraged
and strengthened himself in the Lord his God.

1 SAMUEL 30:6 AMPC

David and his men were at war. While away, the Amalekites raided their homes and took their wives and children hostage. When the men returned home to find their families gone, they were overtaken with grief. They were angry and bitter, and they wanted someone to pay. David was their leader, so they talked about stoning him. Though none of this was David's fault, he was the fall guy.

Instead of hiding, David sought God. He found strength, courage, and wisdom. At God's leading, David encouraged his men to go after the Amalekites. Every single family member was recovered. Not only that, but they ended up with the enemy's livestock too!

As moms, we must sometimes make unpopular decisions. We may feel all alone, like everyone is against us. In those times, hang in there. Seek God. He will give you strength, courage, and wisdom. He will show you the next steps to take, and He will travel with you on the journey.

I'm overwhelmed, Lord. I don't know how to respond to
my current situation. Here I am, seeking You, clinging to
You. Show me the next steps to take. I trust You.

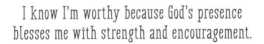

I know I'm worthy because God's presence
blesses me with strength and encouragement.

When You Don't Know What to Pray

We don't know what God wants us to pray for. But the Holy Spirit prays for us with groanings that cannot be expressed in words. And the Father who knows all hearts knows what the Spirit is saying, for the Spirit pleads for us believers in harmony with God's own will.
ROMANS 8:26–27 NLT

Sometimes a situation so overwhelms us that we don't have words. We try to pray, but we can't. We try to explain how we feel, but we are unable to communicate what's in our hearts. We may not even *understand* what's in our hearts. When that happens, relax into Him. The Holy Spirit has you covered.

The name of God in the Old Testament is Yahweh, or YHWH. Some have compared this name to the sound of breathing in (YH) and breathing out (WH). When you don't know what to pray, just breathe His name. Feel His presence. And know that the Holy Spirit, who knows your situation even better than you do, is interceding on your behalf.

Cry if you need to. Groan if you need to. God speaks the language of your heart, and so does the Holy Spirit. Even when you don't have words, God knows. He hears. He's listening, and He's working on your behalf.

Thank You, Father, for hearing the words I'm not able to pray.
Thank You for sending Your Holy Spirit to comfort me and pray for me.

I know I'm worthy because God's Spirit prays for me.

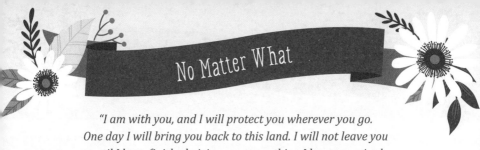

No Matter What

*"I am with you, and I will protect you wherever you go.
One day I will bring you back to this land. I will not leave you
until I have finished giving you everything I have promised
you." Then Jacob awoke from his sleep and said, "Surely the
Lord is in this place, and I wasn't even aware of it!"*

GENESIS 28:15–16 NLT

• •

Most of us have a general sense that God is with us when we please Him. But what about when we've made some bad choices? What about when we're in a big mess we made ourselves?

In this passage, Jacob had lied to his father and tricked his brother. Now he was on the run. He spent the night on the cold, hard ground with a rock for a pillow. His life was a shambles, and it was his own fault.

God's promises don't depend on us. They depend on God alone, and God is faithful, no matter what. That night, Jacob dreamed of a ladder going up to heaven. God stood at the top, and angels went up and down. Jacob woke up realizing God was with him, even in this place. In spite of Jacob's poor choices, God did not abandon him.

You cannot mess up God's plan for your life. He creates beauty from ashes. Starting right now, today, follow Him. Obey Him. He will not abandon you until His work in you is complete, and He's promised to stay with you for eternity.

Thank You for not giving up on me.

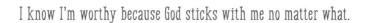

I know I'm worthy because God sticks with me no matter what.

Breaking Through

*So [Israel] came up to Baal-perazim, and David smote
[the Philistines] there. Then David said, God has broken my enemies
by my hand, like the bursting forth of waters. Therefore they called
the name of that place Baal-perazim [Lord of breaking through].*
1 Chronicles 14:11 ampc

• •

It would have been easy for David to take the credit for this military victory. But he knew that God alone was responsible. When the Philistines challenged David's authority, David didn't rush to defend himself. Instead, he took time to seek God's wisdom and guidance: "Should I fight them or not, Lord?" God told him to fight and that he'd win the battle. Because of this situation, David named that place "Lord of Breaking Through."

What breakthroughs do you need in your life? Maybe you need a parenting breakthrough. Maybe one of your children needs a breakthrough of some kind. Perhaps your marriage needs a breakthrough. Don't move ahead of God! Don't try to figure things out on your own. Like David, it's important to take a step back from the problem and seek God. Then await His wisdom and guidance. Be patient and trust Him. He is the same today as He was in David's day. He will always be the Lord of Breaking Through.

*You know the areas in which I need breakthrough, Father.
I know I can't force those victories on my own. Only You can
win these tough battles. You are the Lord of the breakthrough.
I trust You, and I know You're working on my behalf.*

I know I'm worthy because God breaks through barriers for me.

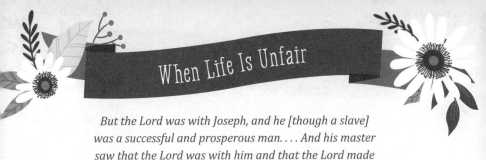

When Life Is Unfair

But the Lord was with Joseph, and he [though a slave] was a successful and prosperous man. . . . And his master saw that the Lord was with him and that the Lord made all that he did to flourish and succeed in his hand.

GENESIS 39:2–3 AMPC

• •

Joseph's brothers were jealous because he was the favorite (youngest) son. They threw him in a pit and later sold him into slavery. He ended up in Egypt, where he prospered as a servant in Potiphar's house. Potiphar's wife took a shine to him, but when Joseph rejected her advances, she falsely accused him and he ended up in prison. He stayed there for a while before being called on to interpret a dream for the Pharaoh. After that, Joseph became the second-in-command in Egypt.

When life is unfair, it's easy to become discouraged, angry, and bitter. But God has a master plan, and He's not under any obligation to let us know what it is. He wants us to trust Him. Like Joseph, God wants us to keep working hard and doing our best, even when things aren't fair. When we do this, He will cause us to be successful, and others will notice.

I'm sorry for getting distracted by what seems fair and right. I know You have a plan for my life, and I know it's good. While I wait for Your plan to play out, I will work hard, trust You, and focus on Your unending love.

I know I'm worthy because God prospers the work of my hands.

For Good

So it was God who sent me here, not you! . . . You intended to harm me, but God intended it all for good. He brought me to this position so I could save the lives of many people.

<small>GENESIS 45:8; 50:20 NLT</small>

• •

Decades after Joseph's brothers sold him into slavery, there was a famine. Those same brothers were forced to travel to Egypt to find food, and they ended up standing in front of their baby brother! They didn't recognize him at first, but he sure knew who they were.

Many of us, in a similar situation, would have taken the chance for revenge. Joseph struggled with his emotions, but he eventually was able to forgive his brothers. He realized that they were only tools God used in His great plan for Joseph's life. He told them, "You meant to harm me, but God planned it for my good all along. Now, because I'm here, I'm in a position to save you and the rest of my family."

When people are mean. . .when circumstances are harsh. . .remember these words. Satan may mean these things to harm you, but God has a greater plan. He has already written the script of your life, and He has an incredible plotline in store. In the end, you'll see. God is shaping you and molding you, preparing you for great things to come.

It's hard to stay positive when I'm faced with injustice, Lord. Remind me that my story's not finished yet. I know You love me and You'll work everything out for good.

I know I'm worthy because God will work all for good.

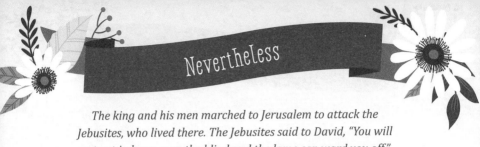

Nevertheless

The king and his men marched to Jerusalem to attack the Jebusites, who lived there. The Jebusites said to David, "You will not get in here; even the blind and the lame can ward you off." They thought, "David cannot get in here." Nevertheless, David captured the fortress of Zion—which is the City of David.

2 SAMUEL 5:6–7 NIV

The word *nevertheless* is a fancy way of saying *in spite of* or *even though.* In this verse, even though David's enemies taunted him and told him he'd never win against them, David did exactly that. He captured the enemy and proved he was king. And he gave God all the credit.

David was called a man after God's own heart (see 1 Samuel 13:14). He was called that as a young man because he was humble and respectful. He trusted God and spent time seeking God's counsel. Because David walked closely with God, God walked closely with him. And when God walks with you, watch out! Nothing can stand against you (Romans 8:31).

Who or what taunts you right now? What situation threatens to make you feel hopeless? Remember you serve the God of "nevertheless." No matter what you face, in spite of your circumstances, God can make you successful. He can, and He will, for He promises to work out everything for your good (Romans 8:28).

Help me trust You, Lord. I want to see the "nevertheless" in my life.

I know I'm worthy because God meets
my challenges with a "nevertheless."

Stay Calm

*She said, "It will be well." Then she saddled a donkey and said
to her servant, "Drive and go forward; do not slow down."*
2 KINGS 4:23–24 NASB

• •

When a generous Shunammite woman offered Elijah a place to stay whenever he was in town, he wanted to repay her. He felt led by God to promise her a child by the coming spring. Sure enough, she gave birth to a son. A few years later, though, that son became ill and died. She laid the boy on Elijah's bed, told her husband, "It will be okay," and set out to find Elijah. She knew Elijah had a special connection with God.

Sure enough, the boy was brought back to life. This woman was able to remain calm in a crisis because she had faith in Elijah's God, who was also her God. We serve the same God today, and the more we know Him, the calmer we can remain, no matter what life throws at us. God loves us. Even when we don't like what's happening, even when we don't understand, we can trust His heart. Like this Shunammite woman, we can move forward saying, "It will be okay."

*Father, I can't imagine how broken this woman must have
been, watching her son die. Yet she moved forward, trusting
You to work everything out. I want that kind of faith. Help
me remain calm and trust You, no matter what.*

I know I'm worthy because God helps me
remain calm, no matter what I face.

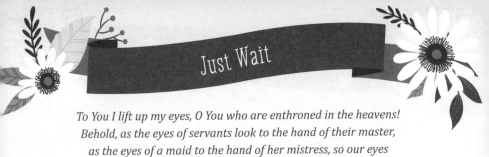

Just Wait

To You I lift up my eyes, O You who are enthroned in the heavens!
Behold, as the eyes of servants look to the hand of their master,
as the eyes of a maid to the hand of her mistress, so our eyes
look to the LORD our God, until He is gracious to us.

PSALM 123:1–2 NASB

Have you ever watched the relationship between a well-trained dog and its master? The dog sits patiently, eyes on its master, expecting good things to come in the form of treats or affection or praise. It's a relationship of absolute trust, and it's a beautiful thing to see. We can learn a lot from this picture of faith.

God is our master. The question is, are we wiggly, impatient, and demanding? Do we disobey, running ahead of Him when we see something we want? Or do we sit quietly, waiting and trusting that when the time is right, God will answer our prayers? We know He loves us. We know He is gracious and kind. It's not a question of His character but of ours.

He wants us to be patient. He wants us to trust Him completely. When you've laid your requests before Him, don't move. Stay right there, watching in expectation, for as long as it takes. In His perfect time, He will work all things out for good for those who love Him.

Father, I'm waiting. Give me patience to trust You during
the wait. I'm so grateful for all You're doing on my behalf.

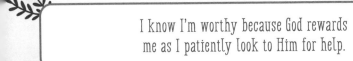

I know I'm worthy because God rewards
me as I patiently look to Him for help.

183

The Touch

Immediately her flow of blood was dried up at the source,
and [suddenly] she felt in her body that she was healed. . . .
And Jesus, recognizing in Himself that the power proceeding
from Him had gone forth, turned around immediately
in the crowd and said, Who touched My clothes?

MARK 5:29–30 AMPC

At this time in history, Jesus was a popular figure. Like a rock star, crowds followed Him everywhere. People probably tried to touch His hair, brush against His hip, or grab His hand. It seemed strange, in the middle of the throng, for Jesus to ask, "Who touched Me?"

Yet this touch was different. Everyone else just wanted to brag about touching the popular teacher. This woman's faith actually caused power to be transferred from Christ into her body.

It wasn't the physical touch. It was the faith.

When she admitted what she'd done, He said, "Daughter, your faith has healed you. Go in peace and be freed from your suffering" (Mark 5:34 NIV).

God's power is just as alive today as it was when Christ walked the earth. And He's still just as moved by our wide-eyed, wholehearted faith. What do you need Him to do for you? Reach out to Him. Trust Him alone. Your faith unlocks His power in your life.

I need Your power, Father. Right now, I'm reaching out to touch You.
I know You alone can work miracles in my life. I trust You completely.

I know I'm worthy because God's power heals me.

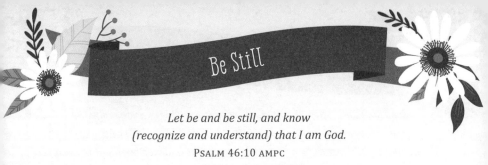

Be Still

Let be and be still, and know
(recognize and understand) that I am God.
PSALM 46:10 AMPC

. . . .

Think about the times you rocked a fussy child. The child's body is tense. She may even kick and scream. At some point, she relaxes against you. When she finally lets herself be still, peace follows. That's the picture God wants you to envision, only you're the child and He's the parent.

Does life have you anxious and upset? Relax against Him. You're worrying about things that aren't yours to worry about. God will take care of everything. All He wants from you is for you to hold on to Him, lay your head against His shoulder, and be still. Think about who He is, how much He loves you, and all the good things He has in store for your life. Listen for His gentle whispers. He adores you, and He will never let you go.

Help me relax in You, Father. I trust You completely.

I know I'm worthy because God quiets my heart.

Stay Focused

The wall was finished. . . . It had taken fifty-two days. When all our enemies heard the news and all the surrounding nations saw it, our enemies totally lost their nerve. They knew that God was behind this work.
NEHEMIAH 6:15–16 MSG

When Nehemiah and the Jewish people tried to build the wall around Jerusalem, they faced a lot of opposition. Neighboring countries didn't want this wall to be built, and they tried to discourage Nehemiah and the workers. They tried bullying. They tried distracting them. They tried everything they knew, but Nehemiah and the others pressed on. They kept doing what God told them to do, and God blessed their efforts. They completed the wall so well and so quickly that their enemies backed down. They knew God was on their side.

What purpose has God placed before you? What kinds of things distract you from that purpose? One of your most important purposes is to model Christ's love for your children. Stay focused. Trust God and obey His calling on your life. He is on your side! Press on, pushing away the voices that tell you that you can't or that it's not possible. Keep your eyes on Him and on the task He's set in front of you. He will bless your faithfulness and your efforts. One day, all the opposition will fall away, and God will be glorified.

Father, You know the things that distract me from my purpose. Help me remain focused on You. I want You to be glorified in my life.

I know I'm worthy because my God leads me to victory!

SCRIPTURE INDEX

About the Author

Renae Brumbaugh Green lives in Texas with her handsome, country-boy husband, two dogs, a bunch of chickens, and a duck. She teaches English and writing at Tarleton State University, writes a column for several newspapers, and writes books for children and grown-ups. In her free time, she does fun things with her four grown children, forces herself to exercise, reads historical fiction, and takes naps.